METHODIST AND RADICAL

METHODIST AND RADICAL

REJUVENATING A TRADITION

JOERG RIEGER
AND
JOHN VINCENT
EDITORS

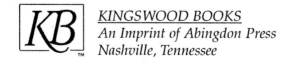

KINGSWOOD BOOKS
An Imprint of Abingdon Press
Nashville, Tennessee

METHODIST AND RADICAL
REJUVENATING A TRADITION

This book is printed on acid-free paper.

Library of Congress Cataloging in Publication Data

Methodist and radical : rejuvenating a tradition / Joerg Rieger and John Vincent, editors.
   p. cm
Includes bibliographical references.
ISBN 0-687-03871-5 (alk. paper)
1. methodist Church—Doctrines. 2. Radicalism—Religious aspects—Methodist Church. I.
Rieger, Joerg. II. Vincent, John, 1929-

BX8331.3.M48 2004
287—dc21

                                                                                        2003012151

03 04 05 06 07 08 09 10 11 12 – 10 9 8 7 6 5 4 3 2 1

MANUFACTURED IN THE UNITED STATES OF AMERICA

To
Ernst and Waltraud Rieger
and to the memory of
Ethel Beatrice Vincent
1891–2000
and to
the search for a more
accountable church

CONTENTS

PREFACE

Can there be a Methodism that is radical? Can there be a Methodism that proceeds fundamentally from the roots of John Wesley and the early Methodist movements? Can there be modern day forms of Wesley's wholehearted and thoroughgoing mission to transform people and institutions that mirrored and received the radical mission of Jesus? Are there already places of empowerment of the marginalized, creation of new forms of community, and inspiration to a new humanity based on solidarity, compassion, and creativity?

The legacy of John Wesley and the early Methodist traditions are frequently related to recent progressive tendencies in theology. There are numerous parallels, for instance, between modern day interests in people at the margins and Wesley's own concern for poor people and his commitment to the sick and imprisoned. Nevertheless, there often remains a gap between Wesley's time and our own. In this volume, contributors from diverse backgrounds in the United States and around the globe reflect on radical and liberation traditions in Methodism as they are lived and practiced in their own contexts. In conversation with contemporary Methodism and the Wesleyan heritage, each chapter focuses on the question of how radical and liberation traditions provide new visions for the present and future of the church.

The essays in this volume, written by well-known leaders in theology and the church, are united in the vision that the church as a whole is best shaped and transformed not from the top down but from the bottom up, by perspectives from the margins. This volume as a whole demonstrates that radical and liberation traditions in the church do not pursue the special interests of a few but the interests of all, by going to the roots of the challenges of contemporary life. At a time when the rich forget that they are inextricably connected to the challenges of the poor (or men to the challenges of women, or racial majorities to the challenges of racial minorities), the future of the church as a whole and the Methodist traditions in particular can only be conceived if—like Wesley himself—we deepen our conversations with the margins.

In conversation with alternative voices in both present and past, this volume broadens the vision for the future not only of the Methodist traditions but also of the church as a whole in new and constructive ways. At the heart of this project and of our use of the term "radical" is a genuinely theological concern for God's own mission in the world, which gives the church its own particular mission.

None of these essays could have been written without grassroots communities who refuse to compromise their faith in the living God, and whose involvement in both church and world beckons the involvement of the church as a whole. In these communities, God's own work in the world is seen in new dimensions, which mainline churches ignore at their own peril. We thank all these communities, located in places as diverse as East and West Dallas, Texas, inner-city Washington D.C., inner-city Sheffield, England, and other global locations in South Africa, Korea, Tonga, and Australia, for keeping us honest. The Holy Spirit appears to move precisely in those unlikely places where mainline churches and theologians usually do not bother to take a closer look.

We would also like to thank David Brockman, Joerg Rieger's research assistant and Ph.D. student at Southern Methodist University, who has been of great help in the publication process and, as an Episcopalian, has continued to remind us of the significance of this project for ecumenical Christianity.

Joerg Rieger and John Vincent
June 2003

ABBREVIATIONS

Letters (Telford)

The Letters of the Rev. John Wesley, A.M., edited by John Telford, 8 vols. (London: Epworth, 1931).

Minutes (British)

Minutes of the Methodist Conferences, from the First, held in London, by the Late Rev. John Wesley, A.M., in the Year 1744 (London: Thomas Cordeaux, Agent, 1791–1836; London: John Mason, 1862).

NT Notes

Explanatory Notes Upon the New Testament, 3rd corrected edition (Bristol: Graham and Pine, 1760–62; many later reprints).

OT Notes

Explanatory Notes Upon the Old Testament, 3 vols. (Bristol: W. Pine, 1765; reprinted Salem, Ohio: Schmul, 1975).

Poet. Works

The Poetical Works of John and Charles Wesley, ed. George Osborn, 13 vols. (London: Wesleyan-Methodist Conference, 1868–72).

Works

The Works of John Wesley; begun as "The Oxford Edition of The Works of John Wesley" (Oxford: Clarendon Press, 1975–1983); continued as "The Bicentennial Edition of The Works of John Wesley" (Nashville: Abingdon

Press, 1984–); 16 of 35 vols. published to date.

Works (Jackson)   *The Works of John Wesley*, ed. Thomas Jackson, 14 vols. (London, 1872; Grand Rapids, Mich.: Zondervan, 1958).

PART I
RADICAL METHODISM

CHAPTER 1

WHAT DO MARGINS AND CENTER HAVE TO DO WITH EACH OTHER?

The Future of Methodist Traditions and Theology

JOERG RIEGER

Methodism in the twenty-first century has become mainline in most places around the globe. In the United States, Methodism constitutes the nation's second-largest Protestant denomination. But even in places where Methodism holds the status of a minute minority, such as in Europe, it has become respectable and moves in sync with the mainline denominations. Even the Methodism that is more dynamic and growing in many places in Asia and Africa often tends to understand itself as part of the more established Protestant denominations. The history of Methodism is often told in similar terms. This is how it goes: Those blue-collar workers of early European industrialization that made up the early Methodist communities in Britain together with the poor and other marginalized groups quickly became upwardly mobile and thus showed the positive influence and success of Methodism. Moreover, Methodism prevented revolutionary bloodshed in England, some claim, because it eventually helped to lift many of the marginalized out of their misery.[1] That John Wesley was quite wary of such forms of success is another story that, if remembered at all, is often told in a moralizing tone in terms of the potential "danger of riches" that has little to do with deeper structural or theological issues.

In Methodism's move to the center, the margins where Methodism once was most active have lost significance. Part of the power of the early Methodist movement lay precisely in the fact that it was not a movement of the center and that it posed the kinds of challenges that could only come from the margins.[2] While some vague memory remains of the margins as the place of Methodist beginnings, centripetal forces pull us away from those margins. Thus Methodism becomes the story of the margins being drawn into the center. The remainder of our concern for the margins in Methodism now usually follows this narrative: We Methodists have made it and we want others to make it too. In this context, our concern for the margins is reduced to a matter of service to the disadvantaged. All that remains to be done is to provide a chance for them to become more like us.

It is not surprising that Methodism has its own variation of the "from rags to riches" story. We live, after all, in a globalizing economy that measures success in terms of numbers, in terms of services performed, in terms of monetary value, and in terms of professional achievement. What is surprising, however, is the fact that other stories about margins and center have remained alive in Methodism. Even today, some of these stories from the margins continue to be written. The story of mainline Methodism cannot blot them out. In this book we present some of those stories from the margins, wondering what challenges to the center the margins are posing today.

---

1. See for instance Bernard Semmel, *The Methodist Revolution* (New York: Basic Books, 1973), 192. Methodism "was among the more important reasons for this happy transition to the modern world," that is, to liberal democracy.

2. For a reflection on Wesley's own development in terms of economics, see Theodore W. Jennings Jr, *Good News to the Poor: John Wesley's Evangelical Economics* (Nashville: Abingdon Press, 1990). Henry Rack, *Reasonable Enthusiast: John Wesley and the Rise of Methodism* (Philadelphia: Trinity, 1989), 368, argues that Wesley's concern about the social tensions of his own time is grounded in having been an "unusually well-informed observer."

Beyond the Middle Road

Usually the center derives its authority either directly through majority vote, or through the invention of a theological and political "middle road" which operates on the basis of a lowest common denominator. Whatever does not fit these categories is classified as "extremist." Only that which can somehow be integrated into the lowest common denominator is of interest. The center considers the concerns of the margins only as long as they fit the middle road of the lowest common denominator. In the racial confrontation between black and white in the United States, for instance, the "centrist" middle road appears to lie somewhere between whites who are explicitly racist and blacks who argue for separation and autonomy. The tensions between rich and poor provide a similar example: the center invents itself somewhere in the vast space between the very rich and the very poor, dubbed the "middle" class. In the United States, most people are led to believe that they belong somewhere in the middle. What brings us together and creates cohesion is the resistance to the extremes. As a result of this construct, the tensions that occur in the middle are covered up and nothing will ever have to change. In both examples, the real margins—those people who long term endure most of the pressures of the system at the margins of race and class—do not even show up.

No wonder that the center never harbors the slightest doubt that its own discourse defines what is of common interest. From this perspective, voices from the margins—if they are recognized at all—appear to represent mainly special interests. The only place the center really needs to pay attention is when there may be overlaps. When people on the margins want what everybody else wants, the center picks up steam and thus may grant some justification to their concerns. But—and this is the question that the essays of this volume pursue in their own ways—what if things were precisely the other way around? What if not the center but the *margins* were able to grasp what really matters? Can the margins once again, as in the days of the early Methodist movement, point us into a new future? This question has implications far beyond the Methodist movement itself.

The trouble with locating common interest with the majority is that what is defined as majority will predetermine the outcome and that any such definition can easily be challenged. The majority of theologians in the middle of the twentieth century, for instance, had little disagreement about what it meant to be human. But at that time the international and ecumenical community of most theologians also happened to be made up mostly of middle-class white men.[3] By the same token, the majority of delegates to the General Conference of The United Methodist Church still do not represent the gender and racial identity of the membership of our churches, even though there is some improvement to report.[4] But even if gender and racial balance were achieved, the factor of class remains. When determining questions of majority it might also help to remind ourselves that while the majority of the membership of The United Methodist Church in the United States is middle class, we do not necessarily represent the socioeconomic status of the majority of Methodists around the world, or even the majority of Christians in the United States itself, let alone the majority of world Christianity.

The problem with locating common interest with the lowest common denominator is that things tend to become vague and amorphous. Albert Outler's often-repeated claim that Wesley promoted a "high-church evangelicalism," for instance, can easily be used to argue that one can (and perhaps even should) have it both ways. Thus everybody is kept happy, except of course the so-called extremists.[5] Worse yet, the lowest common denominator will be determined by those whom we consider to be the major players. If the lowest common denominator is determined in the tension between mainline conservatives and their liberal counterparts, for instance, chances are that the outcome will be used to classify also the concerns of everybody else—even though most people may not

---

3. This little explored phenomenon transcends even denominational boundaries. Vatican II and Roman Catholic theologians like Karl Rahner hardly disagreed with Lutherans such as Paul Tillich or Rudolf Bultmann or with Methodists such as Albert Outler or Schubert Ogden about what constitutes the essence of modern humanity. The link between all those different theologians is, of course, not that they actually managed to define humanity in universal terms but their attempt to take modern middle-class people and their religious sensitivities seriously.

4. See *United Methodist News Service*, report on General Conference, 10 May 2000.

5. See, for instance, Albert Outler's Introduction to Wesley's Sermon 16, "The Means of Grace," in *Works* 1:377. Wesley himself, however, does not seem so concerned to have it both ways; when he brings together diverse concepts such as the means of grace and Christian praxis, something new emerges. See my argument in "The Means of Grace, John Wesley, and the Theological Dilemma of the Church Today," *Quarterly Review* 17 (1997): 377-93, esp. 385-86.

care much about this particular tension. This is indeed what has happened in the United States, and we have not yet quite realized that the concerns of those who do not fit the dominant liberal-conservative paradigm, such as African Americans, Hispanics, Asians, lower-class people, and people in other parts of the world, cannot really be understood in terms of the dominant paradigm.[6] There is indeed little common interest here.

John Wesley himself seems to have had some sense of the dangers of this "mainlining" or "mainstreaming" of Christianity. In a sermon about the image of the broad and the narrow way in the Gospel of Matthew he puts it like this: "Are there many wise, many rich, many mighty or noble, travelling with you in the same way? By this token, without going any farther, you know it does not lead to life."[7] The problem with the center, with the multitudes who walk on the broad way, is not that they are sometimes tempted to misuse their resources, their position, or their wealth. Morality is not the issue here. There seems to be a more fundamental problem: the logic of the center, of the powers that be, does not lead to life and is likely to be fundamentally flawed. In Wesley's unmistakable words: "If you are walking as the generality of men walk, you are walking to the bottomless pit."[8]

If the center is thus fundamentally flawed, what would happen if we took a look at the margins? Here a curious reversal takes place between common interest and special interests. What if—contrary to the logic of the center—the concerns of the margins were not matters of special interest? We all know, of course, the apostle Paul's comment that if one member suffers, all suffer together with it (1 Cor. 12:26), and Paul—not unlike Wesley—seems to have understood that those members who consider themselves superior due to their position of privilege are the real promoters of special interests. This serves as a much-needed reminder that the center never exists independently of the margins.[9]

---

6. For this reason, mainline theology in the United States has never really been able to understand various liberation theologies. Even today, liberation theologies are often still interpreted in terms of liberal theology.

7. Wesley, Sermon 31, "Sermon on the Mount, XI," §III.4, *Works* 1:672.

8. Ibid. Who Wesley has in mind are no doubt mainly church people—the majority of England's population of that time.

9. See Joerg Rieger, "Developing a Common Interest Theology from the Underside," in *Liberating the Future: God, Mammon, and Theology*, ed. Rieger (Minneapolis: Fortress Press, 1998).

In Paul's words: "The eye cannot say to the hand, 'I have no need of you,' nor again the head to the feet, 'I have no need of you.' On the contrary, the members of the body that seem to be weaker are indispensable" (1 Cor. 12:21-22). But does this also mean that we can actually learn something from the logic of the margins?[10] And what would that be?

Unlike the concerns of the center and of privilege, the concerns of people marginalized because of their race, gender, or class always include awareness of the extremes. The awareness of marginalized women, for instance, includes men as those who marginalize. The awareness of marginalized African Americans includes Euro Americans as those who perpetuate marginalization and benefit from it. The awareness of marginalized people living in poverty includes a sense that the rich or even the middle class are not off the hook. The awareness of the dominant groups, on the other hand, usually covers up these relationships. The myth of individualism, at the heart of our contemporary belief systems even in the church, suggests that those who are on top have earned it, that they pulled themselves up by their own bootstraps. This myth—and individualism is nothing else—fails of course to realize how the identity of those on top is produced in relation to others and oftentimes on the backs of others. Wesley took a first step beyond his own position of privilege when he began to understand, for instance, that poverty is usually not the fault of the poor and that becoming aware of their plight might teach us something about privilege and the powers that be.[11] With this small step he opened the way for a whole new set of questions, for a broader horizon, and even for an exploration of new forms of consciousness in touch with the margins that will be further explored in the essays in this volume.

---

10. This is what is missing in Albert Outler's argument that Wesley was a "folk-theologian." In his essay "John Wesley: Folk Theologian," *Theology Today* 34 (1977): 150-60, Outler is at pains to prove that the substance of Wesley's folk theology was deeply anchored in the learned traditions of the church. According to Outler, the point of Wesley's approach was to put these learned traditions into a popular form. Outler does not indicate that the substance of Wesley's theology itself is also shaped by the encounter with the people.

11. See Manfred Marquardt, *John Wesley's Social Ethics: Praxis and Principles*, trans. John E. Steely and W. Stephen Gunter (Nashville: Abingdon Press, 1992), 20-34. In his "Thoughts on the Present Scarcity of Provisions" of 1772, Wesley talks about various causes of poverty, including the monopolizing of farms by the "gentlemen-farmers" and the luxury of the wealthy: "Only look into the kitchens of the great, the nobility and gentry, almost without exception ... and when you have observed the amazing waste which is made there, you will no longer wonder at the scarcity, and consequently dearness, of the things which they use so much art to destroy" (§I.6, *Works* [Jackson] 11: 56-57).

Religion Must Not Go from the Greatest to the Least

In a *Journal* entry of 25 May 1764, Wesley states that "religion must not go from the greatest to the least, or the power would appear to be of men."[12] In mainline Methodism we have not given much thought to which way "religion goes." But a closer look reveals that our normal approach runs counter to Wesley's intuition. Our efforts to proclaim the good news in word and deed tend to move indeed "from the greatest to the least," from those who are better endowed to those who have less. Urban ministry, for instance, often takes the shape of suburban churches and urban strategists reclaiming the cities through so-called "outreach ministries" which include after-school programs, building projects, and food pantries. Through these activities we somehow feel that we are now bringing God back to the cities, as if God had also left when the Methodist churches joined the white flight from the cities since the 1960s. But what if God did not leave the city when the churches left? If God is still at work at the margins, religion no longer has to go from the greatest to the least and a new thing might happen. As some Perkins faculty and students learned when we began building relationships with people in West Dallas, a part of town severely marginalized along the lines of race and class: Meeting God in West Dallas can change your life.

The well-known United Methodist Bishops Initiative on Children and Poverty faces a similar challenge. Despite the bishops' clear conclusion that we do not need first of all more programs and emphases, and that what is at stake is "nothing less than the reshaping of The United Methodist Church in response to the God who is among 'the least of these,'" most churches and annual conferences have continued to move from the greatest to the least.[13] When confronted with the dismal situation of children in poverty, the reaction is almost always the same: how can we help them? This shows once more our tacit assumption turned common sense that the normal flow of things is indeed from the greatest to the least. Based on the logic of the center, even the now common phrase of "working with" those in need rather than doing things for

12. Wesley, *Journal* (25 May 1764), *Works* 21:466.
13. The Council of Bishops of the United Methodist Church, *Children and Poverty: An Episcopal Initiative* (Nashville: United Methodist Publishing House, 1996), 7.

them will not necessarily reverse the movement from the top down and leaves those at the top unchallenged. Mainline churches do not really have any alternative modes of dealing with the issues.

The two camps within the mainline—liberals and conservatives—do not differ much when it comes to "the least of these." While liberals tend to favor social programs designed to take care of the structural gaps which leave people stranded, and conservatives tend to put more emphasis on personal responsibility and character formation, in both cases the movement still is from the top down, seeking to "lift up" people on the margins. Both social programs and efforts at character formation are primarily designed to help those who have fallen through the cracks find their way back into the system. This is true even for the somewhat more radical idea of "community organizing." In all those examples success is defined by those who have made it—and both theological thinking and Christian praxis never veer from this path. No wonder, therefore, that "the power would appear to be of men." The critics of this form of Christianity have had little difficulty pointing out that here God is no longer required.[14] Religion fueled by those who are successful has its own sort of role: In modern capitalist societies those on the receiving end are led to believe that anybody can make it, and those who give to people in need are led to believe that they have earned every penny. Yet God is really not needed here, except to back up and justify the powers that be.

The bigger picture shows similar structures. Western Christianity has frequently moved right along with the successes and evolutions of that which has come to epitomize Western power: the economic system. From the conquest of the Americas with fire and sword in the search for gold, to the colonialisms of the nineteenth century that secured raw materials and the production of simple goods for the center, Christianity has often spread parallel to the expansion of the economic and political powers that be. Now, in the era of global capitalism, Christianity has added a few more subtle moves through the use of new technologies such as the World Wide Web, satellite, and other media, and so—still on the heels of the flow of money—religion continues to move from the

---

14. This was for instance the point of Ludwig Feuerbach, whose argument that religion is merely a projection of our ideals matches Wesley's suspicion of middle-class religion. See Ludwig Feuerbach, *The Essence of Christianity*, trans. George Eliot (New York: Harper, 1957).

highest to the least. It is indeed not hard to notice whose power is at work here.

What happens, however, when religion moves the other way around? Mainline Christianity—and even its critics—have a hard time realizing that this can ever be the case.[15] What would the margins have to teach the center? The chapters of this book are living examples of this new direction rooted in age-old but repressed Methodist and Christian traditions and other alternative global perspectives. The move from the bottom up produces a whole new world that is full of miracles and surprises and where the power no longer appears to "be of men." Mainline critics of religion will have a more difficult time explaining and dismissing these phenomena. Most of them, of course, are not likely to notice them anyway, together with mainline theologians and leaders of the church. But what if God is at work precisely where we least expect it? How could the mainline theology of the center ever have seriously expected that God would hook up with a small insignificant tribe in the Middle East such as the ancient people of Israel, with the bands and classes of uneducated Methodists in industrializing Britain, or with people today whose existence we hardly ever recognize because we have rendered them invisible even where they live right in our own midst?

Yet the new direction of Christianity can sometimes be glimpsed even within the center itself. When North American church groups, for example, take mission trips to the inner city or to other places of pressure around the world, sometimes new encounters with God and other people occur with the potential to help us break out of our religious narcissism. Unexpected and strange, those encounters cannot easily be done away with. A common reaction of the center is of course to ignore the challenge by celebrating what it knows: the success of its missionary heroes and its own generosity in helping others. This strategy still tends to be highly effective and thus the challenge can usually be averted. But what remains is at least a barb in the heart of those who have experienced God and other people in new ways. We ignore this at our own peril. In this context, theology that begins to recognize these issues can make a tremendous difference by dealing with the challenge, by giving it

---

15. Feuerbach assumed that his critique was a critique of religion in general, rather than of middle-class religion.

the authority it deserves, and by developing new tools to rethink the Christian tradition as a whole. Here, theology in the Methodist tradition may find a new start in relation to what is already happening in many of our churches and what is further described in the essays in this volume.[16]

Moving the Center

In the spring of 2001 the United Methodist bishops reaffirmed their earlier conclusion about children and poverty:

> We are convinced that the reshaping of the church and the proclamation of the gospel cannot take place apart from a newly developed sense of community: that is, relationship of the church, including the bishops, with the economically impoverished and the most vulnerable of God's children. God has chosen the poor, the vulnerable, and the powerless as a means of grace and transformation.[17]

If we are serious about this move—which the bishops have backed up earlier by a full-fledged theological argument that includes references to Jesus' own way of relating to people on the margins and to the core of the Methodist tradition—can this amount to anything less than a reformation of the church? Unlike the Protestant Reformation of the sixteenth century, however, this reformation will not be accomplished by a few brilliant leaders. Rather, it needs to develop in community, from the bottom up. It will not be driven by ecclesial and religious professionals and their connections to the powers that be, but it will draw a new kind of energy from our relation with the margins.

The Wesleyan understanding of the means of grace provides a first step. Means of grace are channels through which we receive God's grace into our lives. One of the major achievements of Wesley is that he expanded the traditional Anglican list of means of grace, which included prayer, Bible, and Holy Communion, by

---

16. Wesley's own faith was certainly influenced by his connection with the margins but he did not include this explicitly in his own theological reflections. Here theological method needs to go beyond Wesley—a challenge that has already been picked up by a number of authors in this volume in earlier publications.

17. http://www.umc.org/initiative/statement.html

adding works of mercy.[18] This changes the conventional understanding of works of mercy completely. As channels of God's grace, works of mercy not only have an impact on those who receive them but also on those who do them. We can no longer talk about works of mercy as "outreach" activity, by which the "haves" touch the lives of the "have-nots." Works of mercy become tools of what for lack of a better word might be called "in-reach," tools for the reformation of the church. Here a radical reversal of center and margins takes place that needs to be explored further.

What do we make of the fact that when we relate to people on the margins God reaches into our lives? Even those of us who, not unlike Wesley, interact with the margins still need to learn a few lessons. First of all, the patronizing touch that has often accompanied works of mercy needs to be rooted out. God's grace is not to be found first of all in our status and prestige but in the ways that we relate to others and others relate to us. Second, works of mercy, like praying, reading the Bible, or participating in Holy Communion, become channels for God's transformation of who we are. Those who read the Bible, for instance, know that it still has the potential to mess up the playgrounds of the theologians and the church at times.[19] Works of mercy, the points where God's grace reshapes our lives through interaction with the margins, have similar potential.

The Methodist tradition of the open communion table provides another reference point for a new theology and church. Holy Communion is not the place where the pious few meet in a safe retreat from the world. It is rather the place where people touched by God's grace seek to be forgiven and to live in peace with one another.[20] Wesley assumed that even people who were not yet Christians could benefit from participating in Holy Communion if they were in the process of responding to God's grace in their lives.[21]

---

18. See Joerg Rieger, "Between God and the Poor: Rethinking the Means of Grace in the Wesleyan Tradition," in *The Poor and the People Called Methodists*, ed. Richard P. Heitzenrater (Nashville: Kingswood Books, 2002), 83-99.

19. That was, of course, the experience of Martin Luther and later of Karl Barth.

20. The invitation is well known: "Christ our Lord invites to his table all who love him, who earnestly repent of their sin and seek to live in peace with one another." Service of Word and Table I, *United Methodist Hymnal* (Nashville: The United Methodist Publishing House, 1989), 7.

21. Wesley took very seriously his mother's report that she had been converted when participating in Holy Communion.

If God's grace is open to all and at work in places where the mainline church (now and in Wesley's day) least expects it, Holy Communion cannot be a closed event. Encountering God's presence at the communion table is, therefore, closely tied to making peace with one another—something that cannot happen without those people who have suffered at times a veritable warfare along the lines of race, class, and gender. What would happen if we truly opened our communion tables in these ways? Would not making peace with those whom we keep at the margins and against whom we wage a different kind of war—often without even realizing it, since we may never meet them in person—lead to a major transformation of the church as a whole?

In all these examples the focus on the margins helps us gain a deeper understanding of who we are and of what we are up against. The main challenge for Methodism is not so much the inevitable process of institutionalization or the lack of "relevance." The main challenge is that in our efforts to remain "centered" in the twenty-first century we are sucked into the powers that be, which are now defined by the structures of global capitalism—an economic system that marginalizes large parts of the population and where inequalities are becoming more severe. We even witness a new system of slavery that is even more heinous and cruel than what Wesley could have imagined and more cruel than European and American slave trades ever were, since even people are becoming more and more commodified.[22] The gap between rich and poor continues to rise dramatically, globally as well as within the U.S.[23] To remain "centered" in this situation usually means to find some middle ground—a position that, as I have argued above, is easily pulled in by the powers that be. No wonder that in the U.S. the churches' works of mercy are on the way to becoming big business.[24] In this climate, what chance is there to be transformed by the "least of these"?

---

22. In the earlier slave trade, a slave was a sizable investment. Now the loss of slaves matters little since there are always more to be sold. Kevin Bales, *Disposable People: New Slavery in the Global Economy* (Berkeley: University of California Press, 1999), 4.

23. By the end of the 1980s U.S. top executives earned 70 times the wage of their workers after taxes, compared to 12 times in 1960. In 1999 the gap widened, with top executives making 419 times the wage of the average worker and in 2001 (despite the unmistakable storm clouds of an economic crisis) the numbers were 531:1. See Robert B. Reich, *The Work of Nations: Preparing Ourselves for Twenty-first Century Capitalism* (New York: Knopf, 1991), 7, and Geneva Overholser, "Gap between workers, bosses continues to widen," *Dallas Morning News* (5 September 2001), 13A.

24. The government of George W. Bush has promised large sums of money for "faith-based initiatives" to help the disadvantaged.

In a letter, South African theologian Cedric Mayson wonders if it is possible for the margins to reshape the center. What Wesley did, Mayson argues, is not to reshape the Anglican center of his day but to move the center elsewhere. I want to believe that this move does not necessarily have to be understood as the formation of a new denomination. In the U.S. we have had too many of those moves. But what if we were able to move the center so that the result is not yet another splinter group but a larger movement where the margins are no longer pitted against each other by a center that pretends to be in control of the common interest? What would happen if the margins helped all of us to find ways to come together?

A reformation "from below" might have the potential of moving the center and uniting large groups of Christians in new ways where unity no longer runs counter to diversity. We desperately need the broader horizon that comes into being at this point. The move to the margins does not narrow things down to the lowest common denominator but helps to broaden the horizon by recognizing what holds us together across the dividing lines of race, class, gender, denomination, nationality, by reaching all the way down to our common pain whose global nature is becoming more and more obvious. In view of this pain, new relations can be built that resist the logic of the center by valuing diversity and by requiring those who join in to understand who they are in relation to the pain of others.

The Theological Task

Methodists have long been proud of the fact that their theology is inextricably connected to the challenges of the Christian life. As we become more aware of the margins, our vision of the Christian life broadens. We can no longer merely zero in on some amorphous middle road and assume that this will provide the context of theological reflection. While Methodist theology has traditionally sought to reflect on God in relation to humanity and the world, we now need to learn what it means to reflect on God in relation to a humanity and world which is identified by its margins. Methodist theology needs to be done more self-consciously between God and the excluded,[25] and between what we have traditionally called "works of piety" and "works of mercy."

The traditional resources of Christian theology, including Bible and tradition, need to be understood in relation to who we are and who God is. None of these elements operates independently of the others. Most important, we do not understand who we are in isolation. We need to understand ourselves in relation to others, and here we cannot do without the perspective from the margins which reflects back to us the truth about ourselves.[26] We also need to understand who we are in relation to the God who created us and who transforms us into a new image that we have seen in its fullness only in Jesus Christ, to whom Bible and Christian tradition witness.

The most important challenge in the continued reshaping of the church by the margins, however, is the transformation of our images of God. The reference to God can no longer be the ending point of a debate, as is often the case in our theological discussions. The reference to God is not the final trump card of an argument—it is always the beginning of a new conversation. When we lay our theological cards on the table and invoke images of God, we thereby invite others to do the same and to enter into a process of discernment as to the true nature of God. In this process, the answers cannot be found in the middle through the lowest common denominator. Answers can only be considered genuine (and truly salvific) if they touch on where the real pain is, where life and death are at stake in our own time, and where the conversation is broad enough to include the margins. In this sense, the essays in this volume can also be read as contributions to an ongoing debate about our images of God.

In the United Methodist *Book of Discipline*, the theological task is defined as reflection "upon God's gracious action in our lives," giving "expression to the mysterious reality of God's presence, peace, and power in the world."[27] In order to find out what God is doing,

---

25. This theme is developed further, in reference to Protestant theology since Schleiermacher, in Joerg Rieger, *God and the Excluded: Visions and Blindspots in Contemporary Theology* (Minneapolis: Fortress Press, 2001).

26. I deal with this question of truth in my book *Remember the Poor: The Challenge to Theology in the Twenty-first Century* (Harrisburg, Pa.: Trinity, 1998); see for instance chapter 3.

27. *The United Methodist Book of Discipline* (Nashville: United Methodist Publishing House, 2000), 74.

we cannot remain at the center. Those who remained at the center always ran the risk of identifying God with the status quo and fashioning God in their own image.[28] In a world where the center ultimately remains the exception—think of all the centers that have been claimed—we would only develop another special-interest theology that is perhaps more narcissistic than ever before. We can no longer afford to do special-interest theology for those who have made it, and who are by and large exempt from the more atrocious forms of pain and suffering that affect the rest of the world. Faced with the fact that more than thirty thousand children die every day from hunger and other preventable causes, we can no longer treat the death of a child even in our congregations as an exception to the rule—as merely another opportunity for counseling designed to integrate the affected parents back into the center. We need to ask the hard questions raised by all of those affected by the deaths of children, namely, Where is God in all of this? Faced with enormous and growing economic inequalities, we can no longer treat poverty in our midst as an exception to the rule—as a candidate for welfare designed to integrate those affected back into the center. We need to ask the hard question, Where is God graciously at work in this situation?

In this way, the margins challenge the center's almost unshakable confidence that it operates in accordance with God. The trust that God is somehow in the middle, the ultimate arbiter of the disagreements of those in charge, shatters when we find God at work where we least expected it. What else would be able to save those forced to endure the greatest pressures in our time, and what else would save those of us from ourselves who are used to exerting pressure?

---

28. One of the most blatant examples of this can be found in Friedrich Schleiermacher, *The Christian Faith*, ed. H. R. Mackintosh and J. S. Stewart (Edinburgh: T. & T. Clark, 1986), 450: "Even if it cannot be strictly proved that the Church's power of miracles has died out . . . in view of the great advantage in power and civilization which the Christian peoples possess over the non-Christian . . . the preachers of to-day do not need such signs."

CHAPTER 2

BASICS OF RADICAL METHODISM

Challenges for Today

JOHN VINCENT

Our Present Condition

The arguments in this volume of pieces contributed from a variety of different backgrounds are in accord—or at least in the same ballpark. A group of Methodists, living in the present global Christian community, discern that they have certain elements in common.

First, we discern a more or less universal tendency among Methodists to move toward conformity with the cultural establishment, toward *embourgeoisement*. It is visible in the assimilation into normality—or the simple disappearance—of the distinctively Methodist educational institutions, be they at primary, secondary, university, or ministerial training level. It is visible in the constant pronouncements and reports emanating from the various spokespersons of the central, London-based Methodist Connexional teams (in Britain!). In contemporary cultural terms, Methodism is merely a slightly self-conscious version of the ruling political scene, "New Labour at prayer" here. Is American Methodism (I have been in and out for fifty years!) much more than a hesitant, prayerful conservatism, either Democrat or Republican? The points at which we are genuinely alternative, much less prophetic, are marginal and insignificant. We are simply a gloss on the prevailing middle-class, market economy ethos.

Second, we witness growing moves toward ecumenical alliances, often with denominations that in history and ethos belong higher up the social scale than ourselves. Methodism is not very good at retaining distinctive or alternative aspects of its life, in past, present, or proposed union or coexistence schemes. Often, a certain street-level vulgarity and down-beat, bottom-up crudity disappears when Methodists join with Presbyterians, as in the Uniting Church of Australia. A similar fear hangs over the proposed Anglican-Methodist *rapprochement* in Britain, whatever form it might take. We are not strong enough, self-aware enough, politically astute enough, to enter into any wider connections. Our ethos and our genius will simply disappear—or reappear elsewhere under different auspices, more likely.

Third, we increasingly substitute for theologies based on experience, more catholic "theologies" based on more global or more consensual perspectives. Many of us find ourselves somewhat schizophrenic at this point. We welcome the openness to other spiritualities, traditions, and modes of churchmanship. But we wonder what happens to the more homespun, experiential religion "from the heart" that was the originating dynamic for our church's spirituality in the past, and is still assumed in the expectations of religious experience and personal call required of would-be ministers and preachers. But it is now replaced by a harmless, cooing spirituality which has not the strength to "call" anyone, but which provides a soporific blancmange mentality that sedates rather than converts.

Our theology, spirituality, and ecclesiology followed after, inevitably—and properly. The old experiential doctrines of Methodism—justification, assurance, perfect love—disappeared from our experience,[1] but we kept the myth of them going in our singing and (occasionally) our theology. Thus the British Methodist hymnal, *Hymns and Psalms* (1983), moves far from John Wesley's old experiential listings: "for Believers praying, praising, in trials," for example. If the modern book is, like Wesley's of 1780, "a little

---

1. See John Vincent, *Christ and Methodism* (London: Epworth Press; Nashville: Abingdon Press, 1965).

body of experimental and practical divinity," then the "practical divinity" is banal and conventional, based on niceness rather than notoriety, and using "God" as a label for the well-being of the prosperous rather than the wholeness of the world. The *Methodist Book of Worship* (1999), the last relic of 1970s liturgical revival and sacramentalism, already gathers dust in numerous chapels, our incurably ingenious preachers happily now preferring their own homemade liturgies, even if at the cost of endless new pieces of paper!

Fourth, our theology and our preaching are so harmless! A visit to a Methodist service adds little to life that was not there already! Many people have said how faithful and interesting much of our preaching, leading, and fellowship life are. Equally, many have reported how appalling they are—either unquestioned repetitions of the same old nineteenth-century gospel slogans, or careful quotations from the current *Faith and Worship* material.

We need to reclaim theology as the proper voicing of the convictions of our people, hammered out on the anvil of experience, tested by the scriptures, and developed into doctrine as the way of giving a reason for the faith-life that is actually in us in practice. I have argued that the proper Methodist method in theology is very like that of liberation theology,[2] and it has been good to see how many are now "practitioners" of the gospel in action, in reflection, and in preaching. We certainly need a rebirth of people "living the word," and the methods of People's Bible Study and Action-Theology are now catching on.[3]

Fifth, we have deserted the poor. The last sixty years of Methodism in Britain indicate consistent policies. We deserted the working-class areas and took our chapels, along with our money, into the suburbs. We did well out of the Methodist Sunday School, Wesley Guild, and the University Methodist Society, and became slaves of the middle-class professions they had trained us for. We sold off our downtown, inner-city, and street corner chapels, and used the proceeds for ministry to ourselves. We silenced our prophets and wrote statements of political correctness rather than prophecy. We stopped campaigning, and took up with charismatics and "spirituality." We gave bits of money to Mission Alongside

---

2. John Vincent, *OK, Let's Be Methodists* (London: Epworth Press, 1983), esp. 65-70.

3. See the testimonies and action stories in the series "British Liberation Theology," edited by Chris Rowland and John Vincent, especially *Liberation Spirituality* (Sheffield: Urban Theology Unit, 1999) and *Bible and Practice* (Sheffield: Urban Theology Unit, 2001).

the Poor, but mainly never put our bodies there. We abandoned missionaries and overseas missions, and gave our overseas friends career breaks in England instead. We stopped calling people to mission, sold our central halls, and used the profits to fund ministries of "presence," without people.

So what now?

Radical Church

In Wesley's time, the term "radical" was not used of him. However, the radical strand is very evident, though described in different terms.

In the Holy Club at Oxford, between 1729 and 1735, a variety of epithets was used to characterize—and denigrate—the activities of the group claiming to practice "primitive Christianity," and to be regulated by "Rules"—the Holy Club, the Reforming Club, Bible Moths, Supererogation Men, Enthusiasts, Methodists. The label "Methodist" stuck. Wesley disliked it, but later came to welcome it as meaning "following the method of the Scriptures." The essence of the movement was what Wesley first learned from William Law's *Christian Perfection* and *Serious Call*, which "convinced me more than ever of the absolute impossibility of being *half a Christian*," leading to a determination to be "all-devoted to God: to give him all my soul, my body and my substance."[4]

Wesley seems keenly aware of the criticisms that could be made against such a stance, of extremism, enthusiasm, and so forth.[5] They are very like the criticisms always leveled against "radicals."

After 1737, the emphasis of Wesley is usually seen as being upon "inward religion," upon "the conversion of the heart," and upon the necessity of "saving faith" in the death of Christ, and the "inward assurance" of its efficacy for the individual. The *Plain Account* is full of these, and of the inward joy of the "child of God" dealt with by a loving father. Likewise, there is an emphasis on the "instantaneous gift" of perfection, as of assurance and of justification; and much debate on the manner and degree of "perfection." Yet the heart of perfection remains "walking in all things as Christ

---

4. *Plain Account of Christian Perfection*, §4, *Works* (Jackson) 11:367.
5. Ibid., §7, *Works* (Jackson) 11:369.

walked," "having the whole mind that was in Christ."[6] And it was this element of *loving practice* and *Christ-centered living* which predominated in the following years.

The notion of "enthusiasm" could in our time be equally named "radicalism." The young Wesley in 1726 read Thomas à Kempis's *Christian Pattern*, or more familiarly to us, *The Imitation of Christ*, and concluded: "I saw that 'simplicity of intention and purity of affection,' *one design* in *all* we speak or do, and *one desire* ruling all our tempers, are, indeed, 'the wings of the soul,' without which she can never ascend to the mount of God."[7] Such is, surely, the heart of a radical Christianity.

The concept of "perfection" in the twentieth century became a separate and distinctive "gift," with a strongly psychological flavor. But Wesley's definition of perfection was "perfect love," the model for which was Jesus, and the method for which was classic catholic Christianity, "the common principles of Christianity," particularly manifest in the early monastic writers such as Macarius the Egyptian, who, said Wesley, had "such a victorious faith as overcomes the world and, working by love, is ever fulfilling the *whole* Law of God."[8] Thus Wesley turned to the "radicals" of the early church for his models for discipleship in his own time.

Wesley was a *devotee*, a *dévôt*, and saw this style of wholehearted devotion as the gift of patristic writers like the "Christian Gnostic," Clement of Alexandria. Albert Outler has written:

> Thus it was that the ancient and Eastern tradition of *disciplined* love became fused in Wesley's mind with his own Anglican tradition of holiness as *aspiring* love, and thereafter was developed in what he regarded to the end as his own most distinctive doctrinal contribution.[9]

In our day, we would call this "radical obedience." In the history of Christianity, we would call it "Christian radicalism." It belongs in the tradition of the radical groups and movements, sects, and

---

6. Ibid., §28, *Works* (Jackson) 11:444.

7. Ibid., §3, *Works* (Jackson) 11:366-67.

8. Wesley, "Extract from the Homilies of Macarius, Preface," in *A Christian Library: Consisting of Extracts from, and Abridgements of, the Choicest Pieces of Practical Divinity which have been Published in the English Tongue* (Bristol: F. Farley, 1749–55), 1:72.

9. Albert Outler, "Introduction," *John Wesley* (New York: Oxford University Press, 1964), 10.

communities, which we today celebrate as the "thin red line" of Radical Christianity. Thus, in the recent reader of *Radical Christian Writings*,[10] the story of Wesley's "revolution attainable by incarnation" (by myself, admittedly!)[11] stands alongside that of Christian Radicals in many traditions. Wesley would certainly have felt at home in this company. His own *Christian Library* edited and republished the writings of many within this radical tradition, and his empathy with and defense of "Christian extremists" in his own time, indicated the same "bent." His trips to the continent were to encounter the radical Christian communities of his day, and to learn from them.

Radical Love

The core of Wesley's radicalism was a constant emphasis on the radical praxis of Jesus, the call to discipleship, to a lifestyle of *imitatio Christi*. Wesley remained influenced by Thomas à Kempis's *Imitation of Christ* all his life. But the origin of a Jesus-centered spirituality and devotion depended not upon à Kempis, but rather Wesley's own clear conception of Jesus Christ as both the model and the means of the embodiment of "Perfect Love." The Father is Love, and the Father's love is totally present in the Son of his Love, and to be "in Christ" was to be in the heart of Jesus, who was in the heart of God.

The heart of religion was the imitation of Christ. To be perfect was to be perfectly like Christ, filled with "love divine." Equally, the heart of religion was the service of Christ in the poor. To be perfect was to be totally committed in love to the loveless. Hence, to go for "perfection" without both enchristedness in love, and the mystical union with Christ in the poor, was an impossibility. The tragedy of the endless debate about "perfection" in Wesley's day and since has been that perfect love has been separated from its *core* in Christ himself and its *locus* in the poor.

Wesley practiced and taught a spirituality of Christ, related to the poor. He emphasized equally the discovery of Christ among the

---

10. *Radical Christian Writings*, ed. Andrew Bradstock and Christopher Rowland (Oxford: Blackwell, 2002).

11. See *Radical Christian Writings*, 280-84.

poor, the approximation to a Christlikeness of the poor, and the spiritual blessings to be derived from being with Christ in the poor. Ted Jennings emphasizes the crucial point that:

> By seizing on something so apparently simple as visiting the sick, Wesley has provided the Methodists with a practical grounding for what can become a radical praxis. In visiting the marginalized, we invite them to transform us, to transform our hearts, to transform our understanding, to transform us into instruments of the divine mercy and justice.[12]

From this proceeded the practice of the early Methodist societies— the welfare of the poor, and organization for the poor, so that the poor became the criterion by which issues of church policy were judged, and political policies evaluated.[13]

Such a "preferential option for the poor" was a vital part of Wesley's radicalism. The purpose of the much vaunted "personal experience" or "religious experience" was that the "bowels of mercy" be moved in loving fellow-sympathy with the outcasts of humanity. The grand design visible in John Wesley's sermons and Charles Wesley's hymns was totally self-consistent. The heart of the divine was pure, unbounded love, which expressed itself in Jesus the beloved son, who poured out love for the least, the last, and the lost, and whose spirit now is given by the same loving God to fill the hearts and souls of those whom God loves with divine compassion, which is to be poured out in tenderest pity and devoted, loving service to all who at present live outside the compass of this love, and to all places which are not yet touched by the all-embracing, global, universal divine compassion. Hence Wesley's projects for Christian communism, his policies regarding money in the societies, and his "evangelical economics."[14]

This has been well seen in Ted Runyon's insistence that right— or, better, Christocentric belief (orthodoxy) hangs upon right, or Christocentric, action (orthopraxis), which in turn hangs upon right, Christocentric feeling (orthopathy).[15] And the "feeling" is not

---

12. Theodore W. Jennings Jr., *Good News to the Poor* (Nashville: Abingdon Press, 1990), 57-58.

13. Ibid., 58-69.

14. Compare ibid., 139-56; and Vincent, *OK, Let's Be Methodists*, 29-44.

15. Theodore H. Runyon, *The New Creation: John Wesley's Theology Today* (Nashville: Abingdon Press, 1997).

here primarily the inner motions of the heart, but the overflowing, outgoing motions of the whole person, geared not around their own feeling, but around the fellowship in feeling (sympathy) and the commonality in passion (compassion) which the disciple, the one "in Jesus," experiences in the person of the needy. The whole of humanity is to partake in "the never-ending aspiration for all of love's fullness," and being renewed in the image of God, its original character, the whole of creation is to be restored to be part of God's righteousness and glory, God's kingdom, for which it was intended.[16]

The debate throughout my lifetime concerning what might be argued to be the Methodist doctrines or the distinctive theological gifts of Methodism has, surely, radically missed the point. At the end, Wesley wanted to be possessed by and energized for only two fundamentals—the love of God, and the love of fellow human beings. As he said in 1745:

> I want, I value, I preach the love of God and man. These are my "favourite" tenets (if you will have the word) "more insisted on" by me ten times over, both in preaching and in writing, than any or all other subjects that ever were in the world.[17]

Love, in the end, was not and is not primarily a "motion of the heart." It may begin as such. But that is not the essence of the matter. The essence of the matter is "the love of God, controlling every part." And love is the outward motion of the whole person, mind, heart, disposition, deeds, and practice. God's "nature and his name is Love," and this is the character which is to be evidenced in disciples. "Faith working by love" is the heart of it all.

The debate from the side of classic Methodism is not the futile discussion of degrees of "perfection," which in the end so depressed Wesley. Rather, the challenge from Wesley is about love in practice, about the evidences of the totally committed life, about the radical obedience of love-possessed, Jesus-orientated behavior and communal life.

---

16. Runyon, *New Creation*. See also Theodore W. Jennings, "Transcendence, Justice, and Mercy: Toward a (Wesleyan) Reconceptualization of God," in *Rethinking Wesley's Theology for Contemporary Methodism*, ed. Randy L. Maddox (Nashville: Abingdon Press, 1998), 65-82.

17. Letter to "John Smith" (28 Sept. 1745), §17, *Works* 26:160.

Radical Discipleship

The spirituality of radical adherence to the model of Christ, and the inward transformation resulting from it, of which we have just spoken, were inseparable from radical discipleship, the actual experimental practice of Christlikeness in the world of people and politics.

Wesley's *Explanatory Notes upon the New Testament* makes perfectly clear that the believer is assumed to be identified with the disciples following Jesus, as depicted in the Gospels. Moreover, the early "communism" of Acts is not seen as some temporary aberration or extremism. It is the proper and natural expression of the corporate life of those who had been with Jesus, which continued as a Christ-centered community inspired by the gift of the Spirit. Thus Wesley comments on Acts 2:45: "If the whole church had continued in this spirit, their usage must have continued through all the ages. To affirm, therefore, that Christ did not design it should continue, is neither more nor less than to affirm that Christ did not design this measure of love should continue."[18]

One element in Wesley's desire to have "as much as we can in common" was that if all had the same, there would be no poor, and equally, no rich. Wesley consistently opposed acquisition of riches. First, because riches corrupt the individual, making him/her "ten times more a child of hell."

> I fear, whenever riches have increased (exceedingly few are the exceptions) the essence of religion, the mind that was in Christ, has decreased in the same proportion. . . . As riches increase, so will pride, anger, and love of the world in all its branches.[19]

But second, because riches raise some people above others, and confirm them in the superiority which "differentiating wealth" produces. Riches belonged with power, learning, and reputation as "worldly prudence" which were antithetical to the noblest ends toward which the Christian should aim.

> The grand maxims which obtain in the world are, the more power, the more money, the more learning, and the more reputation a

---

18. *NT Notes*, on Acts 2:45.
19. "Thoughts on Methodism," §9, *Works* (Jackson) 13:260.

man has, the more good he will do. And whenever a Christian, pursuing the noblest ends, forms his behaviour by these maxims, he will infallibly (though perhaps by insensible degrees) decline into worldly prudence.[20]

The model for the penniless preacher was Jesus himself, who "had not where to lay his head." The aim was to build up "the mind that was in Christ" in his followers. Being in common with the poor was part of that aim.

> For I myself, as well as the other preachers who are in town, diet with the poor, on the same food, at the same table; and we rejoice herein, as a comfortable earnest of our eating bread together in our Father's kingdom.[21]

Ministry among the poor became discipleship alongside the poor. Again, the model was Jesus himself:

> Creep in among these [the poor] in spite of dirt and an hundred disgusting circumstances, and thus put off the gentlewoman. Do not confine your conversation to genteel and elegant people. I should like this as well as you do; but I cannot discover a precedent for it in the life of our Lord or any of His Apostles. My dear friend, let us walk as He walked.[22]

The key to a Christ-centered practice of discipleship was "to discover a precedent in the life of our Lord or His Apostles," in order to discern how to "walk as He walked."

Discipleship alongside the poor became learning from the poor. The poor became in some ways the model for the would-be follower: "I love the poor: in many of them I find pure, genuine grace, unmixed with paint, folly and affectation."[23] Indeed, the poor can teach the rich: "O what advantage the poor have over the rich! These are not wise in their own eyes, but all receive with meekness the engrafted word which is able to save their souls."[24]

---

20. Letter to Sir James Lowther (16 May 1759), *Letters* (Telford) 4:63.
21. *Plain Account of the People called Methodists*, §XIII.2, *Works* 9:277.
22. Letter to Miss J. C. March (7 February 1776), *Letters* (Telford) 6:206-7.
23. Letter to Dorothy Furly (25 September 1757), *Letters* (Telford) 3:229.
24. *Journal* (19 September 1788), *Works* 24:110.

Therefore, the rich and privileged visited the poor in order to minister to their needs, but also to learn from them some of the secrets of Christian living. "Blessed are the poor" was a favorite text of Wesley, and implied that all who sought blessedness needed to "learn from the poor," and come nearer to them. In theory, this means that the perfect state was to have "neither poverty nor riches—yes, the desire for other things."[25]

In practice, this meant that all would-be followers at very least benefited from "the consciousness-raising function of visiting the poor."[26] At most it meant, as for Wesley himself, a "Journey Downwards" to be nearer in one's own lifestyle and economic status to the poor.

Once the poor were themselves part of the Methodist Society, meeting their needs became a part of the Society's discipleship. Yet this was not simply "benevolence," "doing good" (which Wesley approved), but also providing work. In the winter of 1740–41, the Moorfields Society's room was used for twelve poor women and an instructor, for carding and spinning. Wesley comments: "And the design answered. They were employed and maintained with very little more than the produce of their own labour." In Spring 1741, the London Society was asked to donate surplus clothing, plus a penny a week, or what they could afford, to relieve the poor members. Twelve members visited the sick every other day, and supervised unemployed women in knitting, who were paid "the common price for the work they do," and above that , "according to their need." In 1743, London was divided into 23 districts, with two visitors each, who visited each sick person three times a week. The work expanded both in London and elsewhere, till in 1750 Wesley "saw no possibility of relieving them all."[27]

In the midst of this, in 1746, Wesley decided to dispense medicines and treat simple illnesses.

> I mentioned to the society my design of giving physic to the poor. About thirty came the next day, and in three weeks about three hundred. This was continued for several years, till, the number of patients still increasing, the expense was greater than we could

---

25. Sermon 109, "The Trouble and Rest of Good Men," §I.3, *Works* 3:536.
26. Jennings, *Good News to the Poor*, 55.
27. For these stories and others, see Manfred Marquardt, *John Wesley's Social Ethics*, (Nashville: Abingdon Press, 1992).

bear: meantime, through the blessing of God, many who had been ill for months or years, were restored to perfect health.[28]

In 1748, he was able to report:

Upon reviewing the account of the sick, we found great reason to praise God. Within the year, about three hundred persons had received medicines occasionally. About one hundred had regularly taken them, and submitted to a proper regimen. More than ninety of these were entirely cured of diseases they had long laboured under. And the expense of the medicines for the entire year amounted to some shillings above forty pounds.[29]

Toward the end of his life, Wesley felt that his project to create a society of commonality and salvation alongside the poor had failed, and consequently that Methodism had failed.[30] Yet the elements of a radical discipleship with the poor cannot be eradicated.

Indeed, aspects of a Methodism of the poor, a discipleship of the margins, are not hard to find, in Methodist history or in contemporary practice. The demand for an "alternative" style of Christianity, alongside and of the poor, has many resonances historically and in recent history.

Stephen Hatcher's chapter in this volume adequately demonstrates how the radical elements in Wesley's practice were reinstated in the early Primitive Methodist movement. John Munsey Turner has written: "In the early days, the Primitives seemed to be a basically religious counter-culture, like the Anabaptists at the time of the reformation."[31] Such radicalism was not elitist, but created the heart and the theology for the Trades Union and Chartist movements of the midnineteenth century.[32]

Similarly, I have argued that there is a logical coherence and experiential similarity between the practice of Wesley as an urban missioner in eighteenth-century Britain, and the practice of nineteenth-century and contemporary Methodist urban missioners.

---

28. *Journal* (4 December 1746) *Works* 20:150-51.

29. *Journal* (16 January 1748), *Works* 20:204.

30. Jennings, *Good News to the Poor*, 157-80.

31. J. M. Turner, *The People's Church: Primitive Methodism from Counter-Culture to Transformer of Values* (Englesea Brook: Chapel Aid Lecture, 1994), 6.

32. Ibid., 7-8.

> Wesleyan Urban Mission is based on a deep desire for the welfare of the poor, manifest in repeated attempts to develop redemptive ministries among the poor. These ministries have not only led to the improvement of living standards, but have also repeatedly produced imaginative co-operative ventures of mutuality and sharing.[33]

I illustrate this from the Methodist Mission Service Center in the United States, and the Methodist Central Halls in the United Kingdom, in which I spent the earlier part of my own ministry, and where this tradition of entrepreneurial ministry among the poor was still alive and well. I argue that different models are with us today in many inner city communities, continuing the tradition of "Holy Boldness," to use the current American slogan.

Radical Methodism Today

So, where does all this lead us today? Joerg Rieger has asked, "What moves theology at the beginning of the twenty-first century—the modern concern for self, the postmodern concern for linguistic structures, or the concerns for the divine and human others," representing "the movement of the Spirit"?[34] This movement Rieger sees as twofold. First, the movement "from above" opens up and prepares us for "new encounters with God's Otherness," "at the points where Godself joins in the suffering of those who are under unbearable pressure." Second, the movement "from below," which is no longer determined by those who are in control, opens us to the God in Christ who repudiates top-downward "control," and encourages resistance and alternatives.[35]

I want to suggest that our argument leads us to a new mission "from above," a Kingdom Entrepreneurship, and a new spirituality "from below," a Discipleship Downsizing. Each depends upon the other. And we will only get either of them through a determination to facilitate, finance, and promote both.

---

33. John Vincent, "Wesleyan Discipleship and Urban Mission," in *Urban Mission: Two Viewpoints*, Mission Evangelism Series No. 5, ed. Michael Mata and John Vincent (Cincinnati: General Board of Global Ministries, 2001), 19-40, 28.

34. Joerg Rieger, *God and the Excluded: Visions and Blind Spots in Contemporary Theology* (Minneapolis: Fortress Press, 2001), 174.

35. Ibid., 195.

Kingdom Entrepreneurship

The model for today is that of the Kingdom entrepreneur. Wesley called his preachers "extraordinary messengers," "apostolic ministers." They were "raised up" to perform particular activities, pioneer specific projects, and make possible particular new forms of ecclesial existence, especially among those previously outside the churches. In the British Methodist Deed of Union (1932), the ministers are called to a "principal and directing part in these great duties" of acting as shepherds and stewards.

Methodist history is one of ever-expanding mission and persistent entrepreneurial extension. Our tradition is not that of the settled, institutional, "established" churches, as static supporters of the status quo. Rather, our tradition is of endless pioneering, constant innovation, and a demanding "work ethic" of laboring for God's kingdom.

No amount of contemporary blasé coexistence with the surrounding principalities and powers of society, culture, or other churches can remove this fundamental missional entrepreneurism from our history. Neither can it be removed from our contemporary Methodist consciousness. Many Methodists would agree with Wesley: the decisive difference for Methodism is not our piety or our theology, but our practice. *What do ye?* is the vital question. I believe that it was the essential question in the New Testament.[36] As we have seen, it was certainly Wesley's prime question.

John Munsey Turner has reminded us of recent examples of such Kingdom entrepreneur churches and projects, as "Abrahamic communities."

> As we look at church history, we see the role of what some in the 1960s called "Abrahamic communities"—that is, groups prepared to go out, like Abraham, not knowing where they were to go "save in faith." In Methodism we have had the National Children's Home, the Wesley Deaconess Order, and Katherine Price Hughes' Sisters of the People. More recently, paralleling Iona or Corrymeela, we can point to the Ashram Communities, pioneered by Dr John Vincent, whose constant pleas for "inner-

---

36. John Vincent, "Outworkings: A Gospel Practice Criticism," *Expository Times* (October 2001): 16-18.

city colonies" or "new style friars or nuns" pledged to poverty still merit attention.[37]

Turner goes on:

> The challenge today is to show the entrepreneurial spirit which fueled the exploits of Thomas Bowman Stephenson (founder of the National Children's Home) and John Scott Lidgett (founder of the Bermondsey Settlement) as the twentieth century dawned.[38]

A Methodist radicalism for today would take our version of Christianity out into the streets in new manifestations. It would be based in shops, not sanctuaries. It would place itself alongside the searchers of new spiritualities and New Age. Its shop window would be the contemporary "big issues"—globalization, climate change, population, migration, pollution, poverty, genetically modified foods, consumerism, lifestyle. Our current Ashram Community projects in inner city Sheffield are two "New Roots" shops, where such issues are raised alongside whole foods, vegetarian, and vegan foods.[39] The shop projects themselves are Ashram's part of the Sheffield Inner City Ecumenical Mission, which has downtown Christian communities and projects based in a public house, a housing block, and corner shops, as well as in dual purpose buildings and houses.[40]

This is not "social work," or "community work," or even "community development." It is Christian community creation. On this, Chris Shannahan is surely right:

> The church in Britain faces two possible futures. We can guard what we have and rely on numbers to bolster our sense of "success." We can be seduced by the "Faith in the City" ethos and set the worshipping community to one side, setting up community centres that have no recognizable connection with the depths of our faith. Or we can learn from the earliest Christian communities, from the Methodist class meetings, and from the Base

37. John Munsey Turner, *Modern Methodism in England, 1932–1998* (Peterborough: Epworth Press, 1998), 93.
38. Ibid.
39. John Vincent, *Hope from the City* (London: Epworth Press, 2000), 99-106.
40. Ibid, 26-35.

Christian Communities of Latin America, and acknowledge that our calling is to be salt in society: a creative and agitating minority bringing life and freshness. Such a future depends on our willingness to engage with society as it is now and not as some would wish it to be.[41]

Discipleship Downsizing

The Kingdom entrepreneur will need to recall that the margins are for Jesus and for the would-be radical not only the places to start. They are also the places to stay, the places to embody new forms of mutuality, culture, and society. The mission on the margins is not to bring the margins into the center, which always means that the center dominates the margins, and either co-opts or excommunicates its members. The mission on the margins is intended to constantly challenge the center with viable, relevant alternatives, so that the center can itself be part of the margins.

So that when Jesus, as Luke 6:20 has it, "looked at his disciples and said 'Blessed are you poor,'" he means that the dependent, footloose, prophetic, dedicated Kingdom servanthood which they represent, is in fact the secret of all things, the kingdom of God on earth, the will of God being done. And this is not a temporary phenomenon, valid only for Jesus' short lifetime. Luke holds on to the radicality of Jesus' demands, even when directing his good news to the central middle-class society of "most excellent Theophilus" (Luke 1:3).[42]

So, too, the strategy of John Wesley in his work among the poor was not designed so that the poor could become rich, but so that the non-poor could become Kingdom disciples alongside the poor. Today, our mission entrepreneurism is not intended to extend the omnipotence of market forces and compliant culture, but to make viable the Kingdom of justice, equality, and wholeness of life for all, in practical, street-level projects and communities.

Ted Jennings's *Good News to the Poor* remains the classic study of Wesley's radicalism. Yet, at the end, Jennings's proposals leave the

---

41. Christopher Shannahan, "Singing Songs of Freedom: Methodism as Liberative Practice," in *Methodism and the Future*, ed. J. Craske and C. Marsh (London: Cassell, 1999), pp. 26-40, 38.

42. Compare. Chris Rowland, "The Gospel, the Poor and the Churches," in *Liberation Theology UK*, ed. C. Rowland and J. Vincent (Sheffield: Urban Theology Unit, 1995), 41-54.

contemporary affluent Methodists exactly where they are now. The alternatives proposed are excellent—a more radical stewardship, equality of clergy and church worker salaries, abandoning our evangelical "preferential option for the affluent," creating institutions for the poor.[43] Yet the one great sign and seal of Wesley's preferential option for the poor is missed—to be like them, to be alongside them, to have an income nearer theirs, to create a new world *with* them, on *their* terms, in *their* places.

Precisely this was the heart of Wesley's mission, and the source of its logic. Jesus took on a *"journey downwards,"*[44] and became a "friend of publicans and sinners," and ate and drank and lived with them. Wesley followed Jesus' example, and did the same.

And today, liberation theologians in Latin America at least do the same for two or three months every year, and hold their theological institutes among the poor. My own effort has been similar, creating a "seminary of the streets" in the Urban Theology Unit,[45] and an inner-city vocation school in the Ashram Community. Ched Myers and his colleagues are currently trying a similar experiment with their weeklong "Word and World" "people's schools" in different urban locations.

Such callings to the gospel "journey downwards" will, I believe, be the prime way whereby a new credibility is given to both the proclamation of good news to the poor and the setting up of the evangelical economies of commonness in the midst of our ever-expanding, affluent, market economy society.

My own experience in Sheffield indicates that there are always people who, for a variety of reasons, including gospel ones, will be seeking an alternative way of life, looking for ways to "downsize," and on the lookout for locations, opportunities, and communities within which they can achieve a more fulfilling life, by renouncing some parts of their privileges, and moving into places alongside the poor.

In terms of mission, we need to add to "you cannot redeem what you do not understand" the lesson of liberation theology—and my own practice—that "you cannot understand what you are not part of."

---

43. Jennings, *Good News to the Poor,* 189-93; and see below here, 54-59.
44. John Vincent, *Radical Jesus* (Basingstoke: Marshall Pickering, 1986), 42-45.
45. Vincent, *Hope from the City,* 141-48.

Christian education now has the challenge, not to feed the global desire for greater expansion of knowledge and experience, but to redirect Christian eyes *downwards* to discover experiences, locations, and dynamics that indicate how the world really works, from the bottom.[46]

Obviously, the "downsizing" only applies to those with the privileges of wealth, success, or education. It is people who have possessions or position who are called in the Gospels to "give up all, and become my disciple." The gospel calls to self-denial, to "lose life in order to gain life," to "take up the cross and follow," were interpreted by Wesley as referring to those who had possessions and influence, not to those who had neither.

I recall a striking occasion when in 1978 I lectured around the universities and churches of South Africa. At the Federal Seminary in Pietermaritzburg, I had been speaking about Christ's call to radical discipleship, and referred to it as meaning a "journey downwards." Quick came the response from the black trainee ministers: "For you it is a journey downwards. For us it is a journey upwards."

John Wesley began life as a privileged person. A Fellow of Lincoln College received only a modest annual allowance, and Wesley's decision not to take a "living" meant that he was largely dependent on the hospitality afforded by his fellow-Methodists, and the lodgings he created for himself in London, Bristol, and Newcastle. He therefore did not need much private money. The model for the preachers was the same. They were "kept" by the movement, and had a very modest "allowance." "Acceptance into full connexion" by the Methodist Conference, in my lifetime, meant basically the same, although the common "wage" was improved.

The decision by Wesley to have little or no private wealth was his own decision. It was for him part of the "journey downwards" to which he felt called, in order to be alongside Christ's poor.[47] In a limited way, I have myself felt called to this—at least so far as consciously rejecting university professorships, and settling myself in the inner city. Yet just such "callings" are needed in our time. The

---

46. Compare John Vincent, *Journey: Explorations in Discipleship* (Ashram Press, 2001).

47. See now Ted A. Campbell, "The Image of Christ in the Poor" in *The Poor and the People Caled Methodists, 1729–1999*. Ed. Richard P. Heitzenrater (Nashville: Kingswood Books, 2002), 39058, esp. 42-45 on the imitatin of Christ and Medieval ideas of apostolic poverty.

world is now rightly skeptical about our high-flown rhetoric and our sophisticated theology. We can safely be left to "stew in our own juice." Whatever we do, we do only to ourselves, so why worry?

There is an alternative way. Get out there and start some new things in some new places alongside some new people. And make a few practical moves with your mind, body, and estate that place you where you might get converted.

PART II
RADICAL METHODISM IN THE UNITED STATES

CHAPTER 3

BREAKING DOWN THE WALLS OF DIVISION

Challenges Facing the People Called Methodist

THEODORE W. JENNINGS JR.

In the Wesleyan tradition, the aim of theology may be understood as "to reform the nation, most especially the church."[1] Without the continual impetus to be reformed, the church becomes only the religious form of the world that is passing away, rather than a concrete and dramatic sign of the coming reign of God.

In this essay I want to focus on two dimensions of reform that are of particular concern to churches in the Wesleyan tradition in North America: the challenge of overcoming mainline Christianity's preferential option for the middle class, by which the churches become separated from the impoverished and come to mirror and indeed to foment the class divisions of the social order between rich and poor; and the challenge of overcoming the effects of erotophobia combined with captivity to what are called marriage and family values, especially as this comes to focus in the struggle of the church to come to terms with gay and lesbian reality. Although these challenges are often regarded as unrelated and

---

1. "The Large Minutes," Q. 3, *Works* (Jackson) 8:299.

even as competitors for the attention of the church, I believe they are deeply related and that in both cases we are engaged in a struggle to turn the church toward the excluded, the marginalized, the vulnerable, and the violated, which should be the hallmark of any movement that claims to honor Jesus.

Over the past few decades the Methodist churches have struggled with the legacy of white supremacy and have begun to break down the walls of separation that divided us by race. This struggle is by no means over. Our congregations too often are even more segregated than the societies within which they are called to testify to the inclusive love of God. The struggle against racism and white supremacy in our society and in our churches continues unabated; but it is complicated by other walls of division that fracture and lacerate the body of Christ These too must be broken down in our lives as Christ has already broken them down through his sacrificial love for the excluded and the violated.

In the Letter to the Ephesians the writer, identified as Paul, speaks of the work of God in Christ that "has broken down the dividing wall, that is, the hostility between us" (Eph. 2:14). I believe that in our time that work continues, and those who struggle to overcome the walls of separation in our church and our society bear faithful witness to that work of God in Christ.

Opening to the Impoverished

Over the last century and a half, the churches called Methodist, especially in the United States, have taken what may be termed a preferential option for the middle class. New churches were built, first on burgeoning main streets of towns and cities, and then, following the Second World War, in sprawling suburbs. Pastoral leadership has been professionalized so as to measure up to the targeted audience of doctors, lawyers, and entrepreneurs. In consequence, the Wesleyan heritage of reaching out to the poor and the outcast has been largely relegated either to those Wesleyan groups that have split off from Methodist churches (such as the Salvation Army or the various Holiness and Pentecostal groups) or has been carried on in a token and largely symbolic way by marginalized urban and rural mission workers whose ministry has generally been treated with benign neglect and bemusement. Even the "foreign mission" work of these churches has been largely targeted to the emerging middle classes of colonialized and postcolonial nations in Latin America, Asia, and Africa.

Meanwhile, the reality of U. S. society and that of the globe has been subjected to a growing chasm between the relatively prosperous and the increasingly impoverished, as well as between the enormously wealthy and the uneasy middle class. Every year millions of children perish of disease, malnutrition, and violence spawned by growing poverty that is entirely preventable with the expenditure of only a fraction of what the wealthy spend to protect themselves from the resentment and bitterness of those who are made hopeless by accelerating globalization. On September 11, 2001, ten times as many children died of poverty as all the victims of that notorious terrorist attack. Yet no one called for a war on that most pervasive form of terror on our planet.

In the face of the reality of this growing chasm between a worried enclave of the prosperous and an increasingly desperate multitude of the impoverished, the Methodist people have been largely immobilized. As we have retreated into middle-class enclaves we have lost touch with the daily struggle of those, even in supposedly prosperous societies, who are the working poor or the nearly or truly destitute. They are not part of our congregations, nor are their experiences of struggle and of faithfulness shared with us. We become deaf to their cries, blind to their suffering, deprived of their testimony. At the same time we feel a growing sense of spiritual impoverishment even in the islands of plenty. We sense a growing narcissism that cares only about its own emptiness and little for those whose plight is so far different from our own. In consequence, even our worship loses its power, for we are confronted there not by the One who both judges and redeems, but by some fantasy plush toy who whispers sweet nothings in our ears while the world around us goes to hell. The life-shattering and -shaping power of confrontation with the gospel can scarcely be found among us, but is relegated to those churches that still know how to live and work among those who struggle at the margins.

In the last few years a sense of malaise has been growing in the church, and at least some of its leaders have sensed that the church can only regain its bearings and its sense of vital mission if it turns toward commitment to the poor and marginalized. Some within the Council of Bishops of The United Methodist Church argued persuasively that the church must turn resolutely to take its place alongside the "least of these," and thus was born the Bishops Initiative on Children and Poverty.

This Initiative, formally launched with a "Foundation Document" in 1996 called "Commitment to Children and the Poor," announced the determination to examine and reform all aspects of the church's life by the norm of commitment to "the least of these." This was then, and still is, an extraordinarily far-reaching goal. From the beginning I have been privileged to work with the task force of the Council of Bishops charged with the design and implementation of this initiative. To be sure, the church has not yet been reformed. Often the Initiative has seemed only a voice in the wilderness. And even those who have been most committed to the goals of the Initiative have understood that the work of the reformation of the church is one that has more often been the occasion of division in the church rather than an organic process of reform. Moreover, they understand that true transformation depends upon the Spirit of God and not simply on the goodwill of church leaders, nor on the incremental changes of institutional adjustment. Even where the Initiative has met with positive response it has often been because of a desire to include children rather than a commitment to the most vulnerable in society. Indeed, even the commitment to children has often taken the form of a desire to include children like ours, from neighborhoods like ours, who look and talk just like our own. And in the early going, there were many who hoped to jettison the language about poverty altogether in favor of a somewhat less threatening focus on children. But determination and persistence have begun to make some inroads in the life of the church. The Council renewed the Initiative; and a new document, "Building Community with Children and the Poor" (Eastertide 2001), has been sent to the churches. This document recognizes that we will never be able to meaningfully address the chasms that threaten church and society in the US and around the globe unless we are willing to concretely build relationships of mutual encouragement and welcome among the relatively prosperous and the increasingly impoverished.

Moreover, the work of the Initiative has increasingly exposed both the ways that we live in separate and unequal societies and the ways in which the church is actually complicitous—older than through all its structures and procedures in this division in our world. The struggle for transformation and reconciliation within the church makes timeworn doctrines of sin and evil, of flesh and spirit, of mission and ministry come alive in unexpected and challenging ways.

Theology is not something that simply occurs in the study or in the halls of academia. It is something that grows out of concrete struggle to bear faithful witness to the gospel in a world that is perishing of its own avarice and violence, its own systems of division and domination and death.

In the work of persuading the church that it must take seriously the state of the impoverished if it is to effectively witness to the mission and ministry of Jesus, the "people called Methodists" have a significant resource in the work of Wesley. All too often, however, the domain of Wesley studies has been co-opted into either irrelevance by a historicizing approach that seeks to keep the study of Wesley from addressing the life of the church, or by ideological attempts to make Wesley studies the privileged domain of so-called evangelical and church growth movements. Since I have for some years been engaged in the study of Wesley, I want to say something about the "use" of Wesley studies, but I believe that something similar could be said of Calvin or Luther studies for the denominations that descend from those reformers.

The question is, *Does the study of Wesley and Wesleyan traditions have a real future?* That is, *Can it provide indispensable help in facing the daunting challenges of our time?*

To this I reply:

(1) Not if it is motivated by hagiographic legends of the saints Wesley, nor if it is motivated by the perpetuation of sheer legends like that surrounding the commemoration of Aldersgate.

(2) Not if it is the subject of Methodist sectarian chest-thumping rather than a truly ecumenical enterprise.

(3) Not if it is sealed away in the airtight compartments of "history for history's sake" academic or disciplinary specialization.

(4) Not if it is employed as a cudgel to enforce doctrinal conformity that violates the heart and soul of Wesley and the Wesleyan traditions.

But in a world riven by a yawning divide between the prosperous and the impoverished—a chasm armed by fear and arrogance on the one side and by resentment and bitterness on the other—the Wesleyan heritage is urgently needed today, and not just by Methodists.

For the prosperous desperately need to hear that their salvation depends not only upon their relationship to God but also upon their relationship to the poor; that all they have is entrusted to them by God for distribution to the destitute; that intimate acquaintance with the impoverished is a regular means of grace as indispensable as the Eucharist for growth in grace and holiness.

The churches urgently need to hear that the message of the gospel drives us out of the safety of all sanctuaries and into the streets and alleys where fear and hopelessness stalk the vulnerable; away from institutional self-preoccupation into a risk-filled movement of transforming power.

The world and its various nations must be confronted with the truth that no law can justify oppression, no government can legitimate rapacious exploitation, no economy or economic necessity can excuse cruel impoverishment or callous indifference to the cry of the vulnerable and the violated.

The impoverished and violated majority of the earth's population needs to hear and to see dramatically enacted the love of God directed especially to them; to the dawning of a truly human community of justice and generosity in which the Spirit of God is at work to lift them from the shadow of despair and death and to empower them to be transformed and transforming agents of the divine love.

And the world, buffeted by manic depressive bouts of false optimism and panicked pessimism, must know that God intends the healing of all wounds, the restoration of the whole of creation; and that it is perilous indeed to defy the call and claim, the decision and promise of God.

If the study of Wesley and the Wesleyan traditions can be set free from sentimental, academic, institutional, sectarian, and ideological chains, to enable this message and practice, then Wesley studies has a future. But if not, it belongs to the world that is perishing; and it deserves to perish.

Overcoming Homophobia

As the challenge of reforming the church in its relation to the impoverished has slowly come to the fore in some circles of the church, mainline denominations (including The United Methodist Church) have been increasingly divided by another seemingly unrelated issue: the question of the full inclusion of gay, lesbian, bisexual, and transgendered persons into the life of the church. It is in fact this struggle that has grabbed all the headlines while the question of overcoming class divisions has largely slipped "below the radar" of public consciousness.

Heretofore much of my work in The United Methodist Church and indeed in international Methodism has focused upon the attempt to call the church away from its preferential option for the middle class and toward a more Wesleyan and scriptural preferential option for the poor. But in other contexts I have also been engaged with many other Methodists in the development of gay- and lesbian-affirmative projects, which also have implications for the life of the church, and I believe for the possibility of faithfulness in the church. To that end I began developing a gay studies program at the Chicago Theological Seminary years ago and teach every year in the area of gay and lesbian studies at my seminary, something so far not possible in any United Methodist–related seminary in the United States. I mention this not to claim expertise but to make clear that I have certain investments in this topic.

How does homophobia affect the church? I do not believe that this is a side issue. I believe that this issue is at the very heart of the church's identity. For I believe that it is increasingly apparent that what is at stake here is the authenticity of the church's witness, the truthfulness of its proclamation—indeed, the identity of its Lord. For in the conflicted times in which we live I do not believe that it is an exaggeration to say that here it has come to a question of the Lordship of Jesus Christ. Here it is decided whether we follow Jesus of Nazareth as our only Lord or have instead placed upon his altar the icons of mammon and Baal, of Moloch and the anti-Christ. That is to say, I do not believe that what is at stake here is simply good mannered civility or liberal tolerance of different lifestyles. What is at stake is the truth of the gospel and the Lordship of Christ. The effect of homophobia in the church is to render the church apostate.

Let me indicate some of the ways in which the church's homophobia is destructive of the church itself.

One of the courses I teach at CTS is on homosexuality and the church. In a review of the study documents and position papers put forward by dozens of denominations, it becomes clear that what alarms the churches about homosexuality is the middle syllable. We are terrified of speaking the truth about sex. The only advice the churches have been able or willing to offer people concerned about the inevitable dilemmas concerning sexuality is "just say no." And if this advice seems irrelevant to untold millions, then the church has nothing more whatever to say: nothing about values to be realized in sexual relationships, nothing about dangers in sexual intimacy. Nothing at all beyond the rote, routine, and totally irrelevant mantra: no sex outside of marriage. One of the many reasons young people leave the church is that the church has nothing to say to them that is either true or challenging in this sphere.

Now, as far as I can see, there are two reasons for this paralysis. The first is that the churches, since the time of Constantine, have been reluctant to speak a biblical word about sin. For in the Bible sin has to do with oppression and injustice, with greed and indifference to the poor. But we are terrified of offending our patrons in society with a meaningful or biblical doctrine of sin. So we deflect all talk of sin into the sphere of intimacy, and make sexuality the scapegoat for human moral failure. By this means for over a millennium the church has succeeded in making people feel guilty and in need of forgiveness for things that are minor (just recall the late-nineteenth-century panic about masturbation), while at the same time dispensing absolution for unconfessed sins of injustice and greed. If ever we were to speak the truth, the biblical truth, about sin, we would be forced to expose this whole shell game by which the church has inserted itself into people's bedrooms to cover its own complicity with the principalities and powers that destroy the wretched of the earth and indeed the earth itself. This distortion of the doctrine of sin shows that we worship the mammon of worldly success rather than the God of the prophets or the Abba of Jesus.

There is another reason that we are afraid to speak honestly about sex. It is not only that our dishonesty about sex is the way we avoid the biblical truth about sin; it is also because we have made a fateful and fatal alliance in the church between the gospel and what are today called "marriage and family values." I am astonished at the way in which the specter of homosexuality so regularly and predictably causes church people to invoke the sanctity of marriage and family. What is particularly astonishing about this is that Jesus is remembered in every Gospel as opening an assault upon the institution of the family. When his own family comes to him, he disowns them and says that his only family, his only mother and brother and sister, are the ones who do the will of God, who are committed to the values of the reign of God. And when he speaks of the requirements of discipleship he even says: "Whoever comes to me and does not hate father and mother, wife and children, brothers and sisters . . . cannot be my disciple" (Luke 14:26). In passage after passage of the Gospels Jesus makes clear that the gospel is in irreconcilable conflict with so-called family values. Yet we have decided in our churchly wisdom that these values are somehow absolute. This is the way that we have tried to persuade society that we play the indispensable function in ensuring the stability of its most basic institution. Thus we honor the Baal of social stability rather than the one who comes to make all things new.

And the human price for this is ghastly. For it has meant that the church has muzzled itself. We are unable to expose the family as a scene of violence and violation. Domestic violence, abuse, and incest continue unabated, unexposed, unacknowledged in our churches because we have decided that we must at all costs support the institution of the family, even if this means we must ignore the teaching of Jesus and the cries of the victims.

Now what I have been describing is an impossible situation. On the one hand the church has determined to reduce talk of sin to talk of sex. Yet where sex really does involve sin in the abuse of the weak and the defenseless, the church is silent. What is going on here? An important, indeed essential part of this devil's bargain made by the church is homophobia. By scapegoating gay and lesbian and bisexual people the church perpetuates the myth that sex is sin while making sure that it does not have to question family values. Homophobia has become the alibi for our confusion about sexuality and our complicity in the injustices perpetuated by the institution of the family.

I have already suggested something of the human cost for this complicity. But there is another dimension of this human cost that ought to be mentioned. Eve Kosofsky Sedgewick is one of the most important contributors today to an understanding of homophobia. In a collection of essays called *Tendencies*, she begins by indicating why she and others have undertaken the work of antihomophobic intellectual labor. The reason she cites is chillingly simple. It is the incidence of adolescent suicide.[2] A disproportionate number of teenage suicides in our society are the product of internalized homophobia: gay and lesbian and bisexual teens get the message that they are freaks with no place in the world. Adolescent sexuality is scary enough in a world in which there is constant sexual stimulation on the one hand and an empty "just say no" slogan from church and parents on the other. It is a wilderness in which there is no moral compass. But for the gay or lesbian adolescent it is far worse. They are actively prevented from knowing that there are other people like themselves who can be companions on the perilous journey to adulthood. They are actively prevented from even suspecting that there are people who have found, against all odds, ways of making sense of life and love under the hegemony of homophobia in society and the church. They are constantly told that the only ways to human self-respect are the ways that are closed to them by the desires that they did not invent, that the ways they seek to find friendship and consolation and intimacy are unthinkable, unspeakable. That they are forever cut off from God and from community by the shape of their needs and desires. In millions of families (church families) they receive the unmistakable impression that it would be better to be dead than to be gay. And multitudes of gay and lesbian teens acquiesce in this horrifying message in which the church is complicit: and they take their lives.

Whoever told them that sexuality is God's way of helping us find one another, need one another, rely upon one another? Who told them that their desire for intimacy with a person of their own sex is a precious gift to be celebrated and understood and shaped

---

2. Eve Kosofsky Sedgewick, *Tendencies* (Durham: Duke University Press, 1993), 1-3.

toward relationships of respect and trust and loyalty? Have they heard this in their society, their community, their home? They have for sure not heard it in church.

Who can calculate the cost of the church's homophobia? Every time someone or some commission in the church suggests that we speak truthfully and redemptively about sexuality and especially about homosexuality, legions arise within the church to cry that we are abandoning the gospel. They seek to silence any voice of compassion and reason, of gospel truth. And if the price of this silence is the gruesome sacrifice of our children on the all-consuming altar of Moloch, then so be it.

Finally, we must take into account the ways a homophobic reading of Scripture does violence to God's Holy Word. The same exegetical tricks that were previously employed to justify slavery and then segregation, and even still are used to deny to women the place for which the Creator made them, the Redeemer liberated them, the Spirit calls them, these same tactics are used today to license homophobia. The homophobic reading of Scripture makes the Bible into the rulebook of a petty tyrant, transforms the wine of the gospel into the poisonous wastewater of legalistic and vindictive condemnation.

One of the most blatant examples of this exegetical perversion has to do with the story of Sodom and Gomorrah. For centuries this story has been turned on its head in order to be made synonymous in Western secular and religious discourse concerning deeds of intimacy between persons of the same sex. Yet the story tells of the injustice of Sodom, which descends to the level of seeking to commit mass gang rape upon vulnerable strangers, thereby violating the bedrock of biblical ethics: the just and generous treatment of the alien. For the alien or sojourner or immigrant worker (all are proper translations of the biblical category) is the most vulnerable member of society, being without the protection of clan and tribal ties. Hence Israel was regularly warned to treat the immigrant with special care, for Israel too was an alien in the land of Egypt (Exod. 22:21; Deut. 10:19, for example).

But from the time of the Roman emperor Justinian, this text has been willfully distorted into a pretext for the violation of vulnerable members of society. And from the Middle Ages through the Nazi terror it has been used to license crimes against (gay) humanity.

This arbitrary perversion of the biblical text has severe consequences not only for gay people but for the church's ability to hear and heed the Word of God. Not many years ago the citizens of California voted to commit state-sponsored sodomy by depriving even the children of (undocumented) immigrants of the most basic human services (Proposition 187). But how were they to suspect the gravity of their crime against humanity and God? For the church through its perversion of the biblical text has deprived itself of the possibility of uttering a clear biblical word of judgment. By identifying sodomy with homosexual acts the church has made itself a collaborator in the biblical crime of sodomy: implacable hostility toward vulnerable immigrants.

Beyond this, a further part of the terrible price paid for this homophobic distortion of Scripture is that people of goodwill learn to expect from God's Holy Word not the liberating word of the gospel but only the mean-spirited moralizing that hates life and despises love.

This is surely a part of the price of homophobia, that the gospel is silenced in our churches.

Conclusion

I indicated at the beginning my view that these challenges of overcoming homophobia and of overcoming the preferential option for the middle class are deeply related struggles. I want in conclusion to review how this is true.

(1) In the first place, both movements have in common that they take the side of the despised, the forgotten, the vulnerable, and the violated. In this they seek to follow the one who made it his business to reach out to those excluded by the religious and respectable establishment of his day.

(2) Both struggles confront the complacent self-preoccupation of the mainline churches in their alliance with social and cultural respectability.

(3) Both seek to expose the hidden violence of social structures of economic exploitation and familist complicity in domestic abuse.

(4) In confronting this violence we discover that these structures are deeply related. For the family is the place where children are socialized into heterosexist institutions; family is also the place where they imbibe the values of social and economic upward mobility and learn to despise those who are "outside" or "left behind." It is perhaps no accident that the Jesus movement which took the side of the outsiders and outcasts also engaged in a radical critique of the institution of the family.

(5) Both struggles as well require of us a serious re-engagement with the Bible, one that moves beyond simply quoting a verse or two, and that actually reads and studies and reflects with the goal of encountering there a living word that addresses and confronts our individual and corporate lives and enables our transformative engagement with the world about us.

(6) Finally, as we have seen, the focus on marriage and family values has been accompanied by a focusing of the doctrine of sin on questions of sexual transgression, thereby rendering us incapable of recovering a biblical emphasis on sin as injustice, and especially on sin as the violation of the lives of the impoverished.

In one sense these struggles belong at the level of "practical theology." But in both cases what is finally at stake is the identity of Christ, the apostolicity of the church, human complicity in evil, and the hope of universal transformation. These are the standard themes also of systematic or doctrinal theology. But they take on new life and pertinence when related to the concrete struggle for the reform of the church.

Nor should this struggle for the reform of the church be permitted to become an inward-looking self-preoccupation. These struggles aim at a worldly witness to the in-breaking of the divine reign that entails confrontation with massive social structures and offers hope to the world's most vulnerable people. In this way the church may witness more convincingly to the vulnerable and the violated the good news of the coming of the divine reign of justice, generosity, and joy.

CHAPTER 4

DISTINGUISHING STERILITY FROM FECUNDITY IN THE WESLEYAN TRADITION

JOSIAH U. YOUNG III

The late James Baldwin, one of my favorite essayists, writes that "Afro-American" links "two currently undefined proper nouns." His view reinforces my sense that I cannot own either side of the hyphen, as my identity falls somewhere between "African" that is, "Afro," and "American." "African" is problematic because Africa has yet to free itself from centuries of European and American rule—centuries burdened with the disabilities of the Middle Passage and colonialisms (both "olden" and neo-). "American" is problematic because the United States has not been the "home of the free," at least not for black folk. The fact that I am not truly American—for as Toni Morrison has noted "American means white"[1]—and not truly African, but in the middle, as it were, opens my eyes. For when I, as Baldwin put it, ponder "the history and possible future of Africa, and the history and possible future of America . . . something is illuminated of the nature, the depth and the tenacity of the great war between black and white life styles."

---

1. Toni Morrison, *Playing in the Dark: Whiteness and the Literary Imagination* (Cambridge: Harvard University Press, 1992), 47.

To quote Baldwin, "something is suggested of the nature of fecundity, the nature of sterility." Baldwin points out, moreover, that it is hard "to know which is which: the one can very easily resemble the other."[2]

It is especially hard for African Americans to tell the two apart because we have been socialized to forgo scrutiny of how we have inherited a nationality based in large measure on our negation.[3] This negation, this sterility, involves the fact that the United States has become powerful in part through enslaving African people, and for centuries. This negation, moreover, also involves the fact that Christianity legitimized slavery—and its continuum in the form of second-class citizenship—to such an extent that many blacks are unable to separate the concept of God itself from their sublation to whites.[4] That Christianity itself has inculcated such sterility is borne out by scholars such as Forrest Wood. Wood argues that there was nothing ironic about the fact that "a predominantly Christian nation nurtured slavery." The tie between white privilege and the Christian faith has been so close that it has been virtually impossible to separate them. Historically, "English North Americans embraced slavery *because* they were Christians, not in spite of it."[5] While I would modify Wood's claim to read *because they were racist*, he identifies the problematic sterility, to which many African Americans have succumbed: "The racism of Christianity has been so pervasive that it has always escaped the full force of criticism, a situation likely encouraged by the fact that the true believer is not likely to acknowledge—or even recognize—the errors of his [or her] faith."[6]

As I have come to understand it, then, fecundity, as embodied by Wood, Morrison, and Baldwin, signifies a critical perspective attuned to the contradiction of black and white lifestyles in the United States. Fecundity is exemplified by Baldwin's sense that to be an African American is to be part of a civilization that he or she

2. James Baldwin, *No Name in the Street* (New York: Laurel, 1972), 193.

3. See Baldwin, *No Name in the Street*.

4. Several black scholars have made this point. See, for instance, William Jones, *Is God a White Racist?* (Boston: Beacon, 1998); Anthony Pinn, *Why Lord: Suffering and Evil in Black Theology* (New York: Continuum, 1995); Lewis R. Gordon, *Bad Faith and Antiblack Racism* (New Jersey: Humanities Press, 1995).

5. Forrest G. Wood, *The Arrogance of Faith: Christianity & Race in America from the Colonial Era to the Twentieth Century* (Boston: Northwestern University Press, 1990), 38.

6. Wood, *The Arrogance of Faith*, 37.

has had to criticize "out of the most passionate love, hoping . . . to make it honorable and worthy of life."[7] Fecundity thus calls that civilization into question because it does not—indeed *cannot*—serve everybody, for that civilization has yet to reckon with its history, which is hardly a thing of the past.

John Wesley's *Thoughts upon Slavery*, published in 1774 and heavily indebted to the Quaker abolitionist Anthony Benezet, whose perspective I will also discuss, provides insight that helps one reckon with this history of sterility theologically. Given their eighteenth-century trade in Africans, Anglo Americans coveted theories on blacks' beast-like nature, which legitimized slave labor. To his great credit, however, John Wesley recognized that the sin of slavery was not simply that of chattelizing a people, but also that of disqualifying them as human beings because of specious externals tied to expanding wealth. Wesley read some of Benezet's works—including *Some Historical Account of Guinea*—and was moved by his well-documented argument that the vast territory from which Africans were plundered to supply the Atlantic slave trade was hardly the wasteland the Europeans had depicted.[8] According to Benezet, Africans had forged cultures appropriate to their environments. Kings and their administrators ruled the territories judiciously; and Islamicized Africans were models of piety for the most part. Benezet thus recognized the humanity of the Africans and was astonished by their inhumane treatment.

Largely because of its tenet concerning "the original equality of mankind as well as the impartial eye with which the almighty regards [persons] of every condition," Benezet argues that Christian tradition had taken slavers to task.[9] Christians, moreover, had set their slaves free *pro amore Dei* (for the love of God) and *pro mercede animae* (to obtain mercy for the soul). Given that tradition, Benezet argues that the Middle Passage was a great regression in the history of Christianity. According to Benezet, the practice of slavery in the Americas threatened to plunge the region "to the darkness and barbarity of the darkest ages."[10] The Africans'

---

7. Baldwin, *No Name in the Street*, 194.

8. For an account of Wesley's dependence upon Benezet, see Frank Baker, "The Origins, Character, and Influence of John Wesley's *Thoughts on Slavery*," Methodist History 23 (1984): 75-86. See also Warren Thomas Smith, *John Wesley and Slavery* (Nashville: Abingdon Press, 1986).

9. Anthony Benezet, *Some Historical Accounts of Guinea* (London: W. Owen, 1772), 65.

10. Ibid., 68.

chattelization in the West Indies, for instance, defied all canons of humaneness. "In Jamaica," writes Benezet, "if six in ten of the new imported Negroes survive the seasoning"—the process through which Africans were domesticated in the West Indies before being transported to North America—"it is looked upon as a gaining purchase. And in most of the other plantations, if the Negroes live eight or nine years, their labour is reckoned a sufficient compensation for their cost."[11] Benezet cites an example—and Wesley cites the same example—in which the penalty for the abuse of an animal was far greater than that of the abuse of a slave. How could persons—especially so-called Christians—so deny the humanity of Africans as to cast them in a category lower than that of animals?

With his eyes on the Africans, Benezet explores that issue as follows:

> Who are these miserable creatures, that receive such barbarous treatment from the planter? Can we refrain our just indignation, when we consider that they are undoubtedly *his brethren! his neighbors! the children of the same Father, and some of those for whom Christ died, as truly as the planter himself.* Let the opulent planter, or merchant, prove that his Negro slave is not his brother, or that he is not his neighbor, in the scripture sense of these appellations; and if he is not able so to do, how will he justify the buying and selling of his brethren, as if they were of no more consideration than his cattle?[12]

The juxtaposition of "the same Father," "those for whom Christ died," and "neighbor" is compelling. "The same Father" signifies that God is the Creator of all people, while "those for whom Christ died" signifies that the Creator-in-Jesus-Christ draws *all* persons together as neighbors through the Spirit of the Resurrection. Benezet's theology thus exposes the hatefulness of the abusive planter who thinks Christ was raised so that the planters alone will live and not perish.

What motivates a culture to thrive on such brutality? Benezet gives us a clue as he writes:

> Consider . . . those afflicted strangers, though in an *enlightened Christian country,* have yet but little opportunity or encouragement

---

11. Ibid., 92.
12. Ibid., 94.

to exert and improve their natural talents: They are constantly employed in servile labour; and the abject condition in which we see them, naturally raises an idea of a superiority in ourselves; whence we are apt to look upon them as an ignorant and contemptible part of mankind.[13]

Benezet thus exposes a troubling relation between self-gratification—the *"idea of superiority"*—and abuse. He is exposing more than economic injustice here; he is also exposing a narcissistic sterility that injures others in order to feel good about itself. Benezet thus turns our attention from the abused to the abuser, from, to quote Toni Morrison, "the racial object to the racial subject."[14] Wesley identified the sterility this way:

Where is the Justice of inflicting the severest evils, on those that have done us no wrong? Of depriving those that never injured us in word or deed, of every comfort of life? Of tearing them from their native country, and depriving them of liberty itself? To which an *Angolan*, has the same natural right as an *Englishman*, and on which he sets as high a value? Yea where is the Justice of taking away the Lives of innocent, inoffensive men? Murdering thousands of them in their own land, by the hands of their own countrymen: Many Thousands, year after year, on shipboard, and then casting them like dung into the sea! And tens of thousands in that cruel slavery, to which they are so unjustly reduced?[15]

With Benezet, Wesley makes it clear that such abuse is an offense against God, and he is quick to use Benezet's pairing of self-gratification and abuse to make the scandal clear: "You first acted the villain in making them slaves," he writes, "(whether you stole them or bought them.) You kept them stupid and wicked, by cutting them off from all opportunities of improving either in Knowledge or virtue: And now you assign their want of Wisdom and goodness as the reason for using them worse than brute beasts!"[16] It is

your money that pays the Merchant, and thro' him the Captain, and the *African* Butchers. *You* therefore are guilty, yea principally

13. Ibid., 133.
14. Morrison, *Playing in the Dark*, 90.
15. *Thoughts upon Slavery*, §IV.2, *Works* (Jackson) 11:70.
16. Ibid., §IV.9, *Works* (Jackson) 11:75.

guilty, of all these frauds, robberies and murders. You are the spring that puts the rest in motion: they would not stir a step without *you:* Therefore the blood of all these wretches, who die before their time, whether in their country or elsewhere, lies upon *your* head.[17]

For Wesley, it was critical that Americans realize that the blood upon their heads was their *siblings'* blood. Even if one had not seen that kinship for Christ's sake, Wesley thought human decency alone should have compelled the abolition of slavery. "Had your Father, have you, has any man living, a right to use another as a slave? It cannot be, even setting Revelation aside." For Wesley, "Liberty is the right of every human creature, as soon as he breathes the vital air. And no human law can deprive him of that right, which he derives from the law of nature."[18]

He ends *Thoughts upon Slavery* with a prayer and poem. The prayer asserts that it is blasphemous for Christians to impoverish those who are "the purchase of [the] Son's blood."[19] The poem is a bit of a problem for me:

> The servile progeny of *Ham*
> Seize as the purchase of thy blood!
> Let all the Heathen know thy name:
> From idols to the Living GOD
> The dark *Americans* convert,
> And shine in every pagan heart![20]

Who are these dark Americans? Surely, the enslaved and the so-called freed blacks would not qualify as *Americans* in 1774. Could "dark *Americans*," "Heathen," and "pagan heart" signify the whites-invested-in-slavery? They were more benighted than the slaves they thought were beneath them. The truth of the matter, though, is that I am sure the Wesleys (both John and Charles) had my ancestors in mind. And what I do not like is the implication that African people were cursed because *one* of Noah's sons acted

---

17. Ibid., §V.5, *Works* (Jackson) 11:78.
18. Ibid., §V.6, *Works* (Jackson) 11:79.
19. Ibid., §V.7, *Works* (Jackson) 11:79.
20. Ibid. John quotes here stanza 3 from hymn #43, "For the Heathen," in Charles Wesley's *Hymns of Intercession* (1758); see *Poet. Works* 6:138.

improperly. Be that as it may, Benezet envisioned that blacks would gradually be set free, educated according to their underprivileged circumstances, and integrated over time into the American mainstream. Perhaps, then, the Wesleys' "dark Americans" reflects Benezet's sense that the slaves, once freed, would not be able to return to Africa, and would therefore have to become a part of America. Indeed, by the time of slavery's end, most of the ex-slaves were strangers to the cultures of their ancestors. The Africans' progeny were surely "dark Americans" by that time. The Thirteenth, Fourteenth, and Fifteenth Amendments gave them legal rights, which—given the seminal role of the Civil Rights movement in re-establishing those rights—has made them (has made us) more citizen than slave. Today, moreover, middle-class and upper-class blacks—however troubled by racism's persistence—share in America's wealth, and prestige. A few—the Colin Powells, the Bill Cosbys, the Earl Graveses, the Vernon Jordans—have a bit of power.

Too many, however, represent the continuum of the abjectness of slavery, especially the black "underclass." They are hardly the shining example Wesley thought dark Americans should be; their marginality, in addition, cannot be said to be the purchase of Christ's blood. Locked into the cellar of society, they are the victims of injustice. Given the cul-de-sac of their social location; given their history in the last century (migrations from the South, where they suffered under a modified system of slavery, to urban centers where life was as segregated as before), one can say that the ghetto is the analogue of the slave quarters.

As an analogue can be as different from the thing it signifies as similar to it, I am not saying that the underclass are chattel, that nothing has changed from 1865 to the present. The difference between then and now is significant. This difference is more than time—the fact that we stand more than a hundred years from slavery's end. This difference is more than space—the fact that the high-density areas, the dangerous tenements, are different from the slave cabins. This difference is more than the distinction between circumscription by one's plantation and incarceration in the penal system. The big difference, the major distinction, between the ghetto and the slave quarters is the violence that plagues the former. Unless history misinforms me, the slaves, yesterday's poor, were not prone to destroy one another.

The sterility of the ghetto's dysfunction originates in the hegemonic loathing of blacks. This loathing is found outside the black community itself and is made all the more malignant because each episode of black-on-black violence fortifies the white community in its racism—as if it were fecund. Society has so criminalized blacks that one thinks that no other people in America will mug you. What Wesley wrote over two hundred years ago is pertinent today: "'So miserably stupid is this race of men, yea, so stubborn, and so wicked.' Allowing them to be as stupid as you say, to whom is that stupidity owing?" Wesley writes in addition, "Who gave them no means, no opportunity of improving their understanding: And indeed leave them no motive, either from hope or fear, to attempt any such thing."[21] As it was yesterday, so it is today: people don't want to be poor and disadvantaged. Again, one can point to blacks who live as well as many of the most well-off whites in the United States. But white supremacy does not cease to be the dominant ethos of the preoccupation with wealth just because certain blacks are affluent. Indeed, asserts James Baldwin, "all that has united Europe as Europe, or Europe and America, until today, is not the color white but what they perceive as the color black." Which is to say: "The Europeans never dreamed of a common market until it was conceived as a means of maintaining slavery."[22] It is true that some blacks hold that yesterday is so far behind us as to make us used-to-be Africans steeped in Anglo American culture.[23] Here, we lose sight of just how problematic our Americanness is, and cut ourselves off from our Africanness—from the continent to which we are linked. We fail to see that our Africanness is not discredited by the discontinuity between yesterday and today, but heightened by today's continuity between Harlem, U.S.A. and Harare, Zimbabwe.

Surely the time I spent teaching African theology at Africa University—a Methodist-sponsored institution in Zimbabwe— helped me process my North Americanness with added depth. Affording me a context through which I was able to ponder a tragic

---

21. *Thoughts upon Slavery*, §II.11, *Works* (Jackson) 11:64.

22. Baldwin, *Evidence of Things Unseen* (New York: Henry Holt and Company, 1985), 81.

23. See, for instance, Shelby Steele, *A Dream Deferred: The Second Betrayal of Black Freedom in America* (New York: HarperCollins, 1998).

*dis*continuity—namely the fact that I am a product of the Middle Passage—Zimbabwe heightened my realization that the extent to which North America is my home tends to change with the disposition of those in power. The sterility of that predicament is owed to the fact that I *look* like black Zimbabweans. Given their own racialized history, I was able to lay my hands on a tragic *continuity* as well: I am still in the same boat with these Africans. With all of us, an indelible Africanness announces a troubled past and a contentious present, which is precisely why I am not an American, simply, but, moreover, an *African* American. At the heart of the noun (African American) itself is a certain marginalization. The insight that Benezet shared centuries ago helps one identify the reason for that marginalization—the *"idea of superiority,"* the deification of privilege. As long as that idea is prevalent, I am forced to agree with Baldwin: "my importance in the Christian world was not as a living soul, dear to the sight of God, but . . . a means of making money" and, symbolically, a means of separating "the flesh from the spirit."[24] Tragically, African American signifies the preference for only one kind of American, who continues to have the force of the word of God and institutionalizes the confusion of sterility and fecundity.

Maybe radical Methodists can help others see through the confusion and uphold the upward path of John Wesley's insights regarding a sanctification that loves God and the neighbor indiscriminately. Perhaps radical Methodists have the courage to reject sterility—bondage to injustice—and embrace fecundity: the Spirit of liberty, of truth, of justice. I say this as someone who is still in the Methodist fold and makes it his business to take notes on the sterile spirit that would shackle me still if I *could* "refrain my just indignation."

---

24. Baldwin, "White Racism or World Community," in *The Price of the Ticket* (New York: St. Martins, 1985), 436.

CHAPTER 5

BARRIO CHRISTIANITY AMERICAN METHODISM

HAROLD J. RECINOS

In American Methodism, John Wesley is remembered for preaching hope and transformation to the English working poor and urban dispossessed classes. American pastors like to share with their congregations that Wesley initiated a unique grassroots renewal movement in England, which later became a new church of the poor that in eighteenth-century America unfolded in urban centers and frontier society. I do think Wesley broke the established ecclesial rules, laid into the causes of poverty, and denounced the social injustices that pushed people to the edge of society. An opponent of the slave trade, he promoted self-help projects, cottage industries, literacy classes, credit unions, and medical clinics to address the dehumanizing conditions of life produced by industrialization and capital.[1]

Apparently, the strength of the early Methodist movement consisted of the manner it blended personal piety and social witness with action favoring the lower classes. The early Methodist societies cultivated grassroots leadership, which empowered the contributions of people who might otherwise have remained voiceless,

---

1. Theodore Runyon, "Introduction: Wesley and the Theologies of Liberation," in *Sanctification and Liberation*, ed. Theodore Runyon (Nashville: Abingdon Press, 1981), 11-12.

anonymous, and powerless. Methodist grassroots leaders acted as both evangelists of the good news of Christ and organizers of industrial trade unions among the working poor of English society.[2] In other words, leadership cut from the same lowly class of an industrializing society preached a simple gospel of salvation inspiring in hearers personal transformation and a readiness to seek to make social life in this world more just.

John Wesley was motivated by a sense of divine calling to proclaim the grace that motivates Christian life and the love of God he believed active in the world. One hardly needs reminding that Wesley desired to deepen the religious life of members of the Anglican church, but was met with opposition. Nonetheless, he strategically turned to the world of the poor and forgotten of his time. What at first was a strategic response of going to the margins of society yielded to the far more important insight that the gospel leads Christians to see the world of the poor, vulnerable, and disinherited as the ultimate context of Christian revelation. Wesley did not blame poverty on idleness; instead, the misery of the masses prompted in him a deep concern for the needs of the deprived and an understanding that poverty goes with joblessness and the interrelated problems of capital.[3]

Wesley's basic theological intuition also affirmed the rights of black humanity and to a lesser extent those of women, although he resisted supporting revolutionary political change. Nonetheless, Wesley's solidarity with the poor and practices associated with his movement on their behalf speak to us now of the importance of hearing the cries of this vast majority of humanity. That Wesley opted for the poor reminds us today to view poverty as systemically linked to the economic and political policies that deprive people of livable work, health care, nutrition, shelter, education, dignity, and human rights. Wesley's solidarity with the margins even now reminds Methodists in American society not to regard the poor as welfare cheats, drug abusers, illegal aliens, undeserving, and dishonest.

In my view, the steady upward class mobility experienced by members of the Methodist Church in the States and the concern to

---

2. Guillermo Cook, *The Expectation of the Poor: Latin American Basic Ecclesial Communities in Protestant Perspective* (Maryknoll: Orbis Books, 1985), 184.

3. Thomas W. Madron, "John Wesley on Economics," in *Sanctification and Liberation*, 111.

win over the upper and middle classes by denominational leaders resulted in a waning concern for the very poor that directed the sympathy and evangelical energy of John Wesley and his movement. For the most part, American Methodism lost touch with the working class and poor of society as it pursued ecclesial maturity and institutional stability; however, with the appearance of Central American newcomers in American society the renewal of Christian witness is starting to flow from the barrio into Methodist congregations, a development which promises to help the entire church reevaluate the meaning of discipleship. The faith in the God of life expressed now by Central Americans in the barrio may very well be a proper development of Wesley's own identification with the poor and practical discipleship.[4]

Barrio Christians place the church in tension with the values of the wider dominant culture. Latino/a newcomers like Salvadorans are well aware that the preferences, practices, and care of the One who was born in the stench of a stable, died on the wood of the cross, and was raised by God directs the entire church to model radical discipleship in the world.[5] The emerging new barrio Christianity advocates the view that radical discipleship acknowledges: God saves in history by delivering human beings from death to life, darkness to light, fatalism to struggle, and from the cross to resurrection. In my work with Salvadorans in the barrio, I discovered that radical discipleship also included nothing less than confronting the established church's distorted theological view of God ruling in almighty power and trampling the poor.

When barrio congregations rethink their faith from the margins of society, they affirm that Christian witness means reading the scriptures from the perspective of the poor, the sharing of life-story testimonies of liberation, and the commitment to struggle with social nobodies for justice in the world. As American Methodism

---

4. Generally, Wesley is associated with the politics of social reformism. Today, he inspires the view that the basic political and economic structures of liberal capitalist society require humanization, not radical change. Meanwhile, the radical witness of Latino/a newcomers to the barrio blames liberal democratic and capitalist society for the misery of the poor. Thus, radical discipleship here implies a need to honor democratic institutions in the context of activity geared toward the radical restructuring of economic and social conditions of life.

5. Radical discipleship means living compassionately toward the poor by engaging in activity directed toward the transformation of the life-denying structures that determine human experience at the margins of society, especially economic, political, ideological, and cultural structures.

enters into conversation with this barrio church it will discover anew that faith called to radical discipleship begins with Jesus Christ, who committed himself to bring good news to the poor and justice into a broken world. I think the renewal of American Methodism will be helped along when mainstream congregations relate to barrio Christians who confess that Jesus is a source of resistance to oppression, a light that opens a path to a new humanity and a transforming power before crucifying reality.

American Methodism will especially find that Salvadorans in the barrio are a group of Christians who follow Jesus to bring to fullness the peace and justice promised by the gospel. In part, this means keeping American Methodist theology from being exclusively dominated by intellectual and economic elites who limit Christian social, economic, and political criticism of national life and global practices. The radical discipleship advocated now in a growing number of barrio congregations centers Christian witness in the God of life, the cross of Jesus, and the resurrection of the illiterate peasant who announced the coming of a just society for all human beings. American Methodism will rekindle its weakened radical Wesleyan tradition by pursuing with Salvadorans in the barrio a spirituality awake to the reality of oppressed-suffering, the structure of sin in the world, and the transforming possibilities of God's encompassing love for human beings.

In my experience, Salvadorans associating with Methodist churches in the barrio often question why church members are tentative about taking a public stance against the systems of economic and political life that produce victims in order to survive. In this sense, they critique from the margins of society the standard expressions of Methodist congregations that mostly bear witness to a God that ignores the situation of the poor by keeping silent and politically inactive in the face of crucifying realities. Barrio Christians recognize that when faith is lived in a process of liberation in the context of real social and political conflict, a new level of theological depth and practice can be expected to issue forth in the life of the church. Salvadorans will tell you that nothing is more necessary for the renewal of radical discipleship in Methodism than a genuine surrender to the God of compassion who favors trampled people.

Salvadorans now show the American Methodist church what it should become by inviting it to a complete immersion in the wretched conditions of the poor found in the barrio. The suffering of Christ in history continues in the situation of economic exploitation, racial humiliation, and oppression known by Latinos in the barrio. In the barrio, Latinos and Latinas rely on their faith in the God of life, who absolutely contradicts the dehumanizing and troubled present, to plead their cause for justice and work for a new life. I think that through the witness of Salvadorans and other Central Americans in the barrio, Methodists will learn to affirm that the mission of the church makes a practical difference when crucified reality is raised to the level of theological concept; indeed, the present reality of the barrio suggests that the church finds its authentic meaning by not abandoning the poor and the commitment to change the system which causes poverty and desolation.

Whether out of ignorance or design, the American Methodist church has largely overlooked the Latino/a world of the barrio—except when questioning its church leaders for not harboring a mainstream white middle-class theology. In what follows, I propose to examine the contributions of the Latino/a margin in light of its promise to renew and radicalize the meaning of discipleship for American Methodism. I believe that by entering into a profound and fruitful cross-cultural dialogue with rejected and despised people, Methodism will escape from its fatal identification with a theology of power and a practice of indifference to the poor and oppressed. Hence, I will discuss below four contributions from the Latino/a margin: (1) the God of Life, (2) the Cross of Jesus, (3) the Church of the Poor, and (4) Voices from the Margin.

The God of Life

A vicious civil war in El Salvador (1980–1992) caused a massive flight of people from that country into barrios in the United States. They came sharing stories about violence and death in El Salvador, but like Paul, could say: "They treat us as liars, although we speak the truth; they regard us as strangers, although we are well known. We are half-dead, but we continue to live; they punish us, but they have not killed us" (2 Cor. 6:8-9 NVI/NIV Biblia Bilingüe).

Although Salvadorans were crying in the barrio wilderness for an end to the civil war and U.S. support of it, American Methodist congregations mostly did not listen or denied what was heard. American Methodism failed to understand that God was incarnate in the barrio in Salvadoran refugees through whom God was finding a loud voice, a persecuted face, and a cause to defend in our time.

In the barrio, Salvadorans renew faith in the God of life in the midst of poverty, hunger, desperation, conflict, civil strife, doubt, fear, violence, betrayal, and death. Through them, barrio churches focus on a God of life who acts in history in human efforts that bring freedom, justice, equality, and solidarity. In one mostly Salvadoran Methodist congregation in the nation's capital, the Lord's Prayer is especially invoked to direct persons' attention to a spirituality of hope born in the struggle for life. For members of this little Salvadoran church, Jesus' prayer describes the in-breaking reign of God in the midst of misery and crucified existence, especially offering a promise of life-sustaining bread. These barrio Christians understand that in praying for daily bread, one commits to share with others. Salvadorans say that the God of life who defends the cause of the poor demands that the church break bread with those in society who are denied room to be human beings.

The Lord's Prayer reveals a God of life who permits the hungry to pluck grain from another's field to meet basic human needs. For Salvadorans this prayer suggests that God will not be God without liberating the bruised of society from misery and want. One Salvadoran woman, Marisol, who escaped the violence of the civil war shared that the God at the center of the Lord's Prayer delivered her from death so she could speak the truth to power and play a role in ending the war in El Salvador. For her, saying the Lord's Prayer meant engaging in an ongoing conversion to compassion for the hungry, the struggle to create a better life, and solidarity with people in need. Praying for daily bread and the courage to do the will of God in this conflicted world, meant for her loving the least and questioning the structure of sin in the world. Marisol prayed Jesus' prayer out of a basic theological intuition of the margin: the God of life always gives more than the present allows—bread is life and a denial of death.

Salvadoran newcomers to local Methodist congregations in the barrio believe that the God of life is displeased with the conditions of Latino/a life where people exist on the edge of survival and with a minimum of dignity. They proclaim that the God of life opposes the systemic forces that cause too many Latino/a youths to be shaped by social pathologies like youth homicide, teen pregnancy, drug abuse, gang violence, the medical epidemic of AIDS, poverty, and oppression. In their desire to be faithful to the gospel, Salvadoran newcomers to barrio congregations declare that the God of life demands a change in the basic socioeconomic models and human values that create structures which permit the wealthy to take life for granted as the poor slip into a world of misery and die on the killing sidewalks of an uncaring society.

More and more, barrio Christians are critical of American Methodism for failing to address the basic human rights of the poor or to support the victims of power in history (Luke 10:25-37). They believe that the church needs to be converted to a radical discipleship that admits that the God of life is revealed in the concrete world of the rejected. They believe that the church must be a space that overcomes human enmity and welcomes strangers with love. Salvadorans know that from the position of solidarity with the vulnerable, American Methodism can reclaim its radical tradition and confess the living God who values the service of truth and love over power and domination. Once American Methodism moves away from theology as an idealistic activity to encounter the barrio, it will joyfully proclaim that God is doing a new thing with the humiliated and hungry (Luke 1:52-53).

One Salvadoran woman named Emilia, a member of a Methodist church in New York City, remarked that the God of life at the center of her faith does not offer people a gospel of submission; instead, "the good news of God is liberation and naming reality." For her, belief in the God of life and in the good news implies that the church's task is not simply to guide people in religious matters, but to address the real-life problems faced by them, to offer a liberating evangelization, to take seriously the political vocation of discipleship. Emilia believes that a church that confesses the God of life politically represents the Word of God in the world by accompanying the poor through affirmation of their positive values, struggles, and hopes for social change. According to Emilia, mainline churches need to pray for that daily bread that nourishes the view that God is present in the Latino/a struggle against poverty and injustice.[6]

The Cross of Jesus

American Methodism encounters humble people in the barrio sharing their ideas about God, Christ, sin, salvation, politics, church, morality, and life. In the barrio context, Latinos and Latinas know that love for God requires taking up the cross of Jesus to confront the concrete situations of life. Mainstream Methodism will especially find that for Salvadorans in the barrio, following Jesus implies taking seriously a theology and ethics of martyrdom. Salvadoran faith is shaped by a martyrial theology of Christian witness, which associates Christian discipleship with losing one's life for the poor or crucified people in order to achieve a democratized state, a demilitarized society, economic justice, and the realization of human rights.[7] Thus, it should not surprise us that in the barrio today a liberative theology of the cross points the way toward a radicalized American Methodism.

Salvadorans understand that Jesus' suffering and violent death on the cross speak directly to their world of poverty, marginality, and struggle. Through them, U.S.-based Latino/a Christians are learning to revisit the view that Jesus was crucified by powerful religious and political leaders, a view which serves to motivate a faith witness opposed to institutionalized violence and death. Salvadoran newcomers to barrio churches link the terrifying cross of Jesus of Nazareth with the history of the slaughter of the poor in their country's brutal civil war and in violence on the barrio streets; moreover, they relate the crucified Lord to the realities found by people who live in U.S. barrios and who cry out for justice. Their witness to the cross implies action that seeks the liberation of people from exploitation, exclusion, marginality, and the structures that deny life.

---

6. Central Americans in the United States add their voice to the production of theology and remind even the U.S. Hispanic community that the common themes and issues of Hispanic theology are not only conquest, *mestizaje*, gender, class, and the engagement of popular religion as a theological source, but faith flowing from struggles for survival, justice, liberation, and dignified life.

7. Harold J. Recinos, *Who Comes in the Name of the Lord? Jesus at the Margins* (Nashville: Abingdon Press, 1997), 97.

For Salvadorans in the barrio, the cross is a reminder of their world, where men and women died like Jesus: arrested in the middle of the night, tortured, and crucified for the sake of forgotten people. In Salvadoran barrio enclaves, crosses are everywhere displayed in contexts outside the church, such as legal services agencies, restaurants, sport-viewing pubs, homes, and around people's necks. The cross of Jesus is not only a reminder of the permanent presence of the divine in daily life, but is also a lens for understanding the activity of God incarnate in the world of the abused, tortured, beaten, rejected, and lifeless. Salvadorans do not debate the idea that the cross is a consequence of Jesus' preaching of good news to the poor, freedom from dividing hostilities, and solidarity with beaten-down persons; more importantly, the cross points the church toward the victims of history whose flesh reveals the structures that kill in society.

From the barrio, Salvadorans tell us that the cross reveals God in the history of people rendered poor by unjust power and economic structures. For Salvadorans, the crucified Jesus who entered and left the world in rejected status personally knows what it is like to live lacking bread, justice, freedom, equality, and abundant life. Thus, Salvadorans speak of the cross in terms of God's nearness to human suffering and vulnerability in the face of human cruelty. This translates in barrio congregations as walking with the crucified Jesus in terms of a commitment to those in need whom God preferentially loves (Matt. 25:31-46; Luke 4:18-21). At the practical level, it means barrio Methodism is now slowly admitting that the crucified Jesus requires the whole church to radically deny itself by shouldering the cross of those who suffer and by seeking the joy of their resurrection .

More and more, barrio Christians find in the cross freedom from imprisonment in a private religion that is useless for overcoming problems in public life. Barrio churches under the sign of the cross render service to the Crucified Lord in the world by acting against the structures that keep the weakest members of society from having life and having it more abundantly (John 10:10). Today, the crucified people of the barrio plea for the entire church to recognize that the cross resulted from Jesus' questioning of the conformist power of mainline religious leaders, which was used to support death-dealing cultural, ideological, economic, political, and social structures. Salvadorans will ultimately say that the entire church may not deny that the cross moves us away from suffering and death toward justice and life.

Salvadorans tell us that Jesus got in the way of social groups who brought injustice and death to the poor through systemic domination; indeed, pious religious leaders convicted Jesus in the name of a violent God, while Roman political leaders had him nailed to a cross. But Salvadorans will also say that the cross reflects the fact that Jesus was obedient unto death and was always compassionate toward the bruised of society. He preached the nearness of the reign of God and demonstrated its presence in an atmosphere of mounting persecution and finally death. Jesus' fears did not prevent him from serving the God of life who offers forgiveness to an estranged and godless world. Jesus brought God to human beings by way of a cross that exposes the vulnerable love of a God who meets sinful human beings with open arms and a promise of new life.

Ultimately, barrio Christians are now saying more loudly that God is acutely present in the condemned of history. God rejects executioners and raises their victims.[8] I think that Salvadorans in the barrio context invite American Methodists to carry the cross of Jesus by staying close to human suffering. Only by remaining close to places of crucifixion in the world will the church fully understand the meaning of radical discipleship. The crucified people of the world keep the church awake in the gospel of Jesus Christ. The God who suffers on the cross and in our suffering world shows the church that redemption begins in the setting of the powerless. What barrio Christians know for certain is that the death of Jesus and his ongoing daily crucifixion yields to a message of life—"the risen One is Jesus of Nazareth, who was crucified" (Mark 16:6 NVI/NIV Biblia Bilingüe).

The Church of the Poor

In Latin America a new way of being the church in the world was born among despised ethnic groups and the rejected poor; indeed, the existential circumstances of this subdivision of society

---

8. See especially Jon Sobrino, *Jesus the Liberator: A Historical-Theological View* (Maryknoll: Orbis Books, 1993).

kept alive the ethical demands of the gospel and the question of God in a sinful world. In this new church of the poor, Jesus presents himself with the wounds of his crucifixion in the faces of the vast majority of people who live and die exploited, oppressed, and seeking a better understanding of the parenthood of God and the kinship of all people.[9] Here again, from the barrio, Salvadorans who helped to build this new church of the poor in their native country call on mainstream Christians to elect a life of solidarity with the margins by becoming good news.

In my view, a new church of the poor is emerging in the barrio through Salvadoran Christians who celebrate a biblical faith that declares that God "executes justice for the fatherless and the widow, and loves sojourners, giving them food and clothing" (Deut. 10:18 NVI/NIV Biblia Bilingüe). From this emerging church of the poor, the risen Lord confronts the false gods that operate in American Methodism and that assure the idolization of wealth and structural violence toward the poor. Today, the barrio poor who determine what is ultimate for Christianity declare from their world of dehumanizing economic misery that they are loved preferentially by God. Moreover, these Latino/a Christians hear God saying to the more privileged sectors of the church, "You may multiply your prayers, I shall not listen. Your hands are covered with blood" (Isa. 1:15 NVI/NIV Biblia Bilingüe).

I have listened to Salvadorans observe that American Methodists would rather flee from changing urban communities to white suburbs than support the building of churches in the barrio that address real problems. At best, the American Methodist commitment to the world of the poor in the barrio finds expression in the provision of social assistance projects, while the causes of economic inequality and political powerlessness remain unexamined. Ironically, American Methodism seeks to evangelize in the Latino/a community—that is, to promote the establishment of faith communities and new church starts—but its largely self-serving church-growth orientation is blind to the unfolding new church experience in the barrio. The emerging church of the poor understands that the truth and practice of the gospel requires establishing

---

9. See Jon Sobrino, "The Church of the Poor," in *The True Church and the Poor* (Maryknoll: Orbis Books, 1984), 84-124. Also see Gustavo Gutierrez, "Theology from the Underside of History," in *The Power of the Poor in History*, trans. Robert R. Barr (Maryknoll: Orbis Books, 1983), 169-221.

congregations that confront dominant political and economic orders, not building more liturgical communities.

With Salvadorans in the barrio, I have discovered that the true wealth of the church consists of its becoming an institution of good news. Members of one church in Washington, D.C., where I served as a senior pastor while on the faculty of a Methodist seminary, think American Methodism needs to be emptied of the superiority complex that keeps it from living the gospel. American Methodism must give up its privileged life for the sake of the crucified through whom it truly gains life. In the barrio, the new church of the poor believes that solidarity and struggle with people at the margins needs to become the foundation of American Methodism's self-emptying process (kenosis). One Salvadoran, Ramiro, insightfully remarked:

> The purpose of the church of the poor is that it identifies that Christ was poor, he was persecuted, assassinated, and raised from the dead. The church of the poor takes this example and decides to be like Christ who struggled for all people to have the right to exist, for a world that does not disgrace and abuse human beings.[10]

Regrettably, American Methodist churches are so preoccupied with church-growth schemes that they confuse organizational development with commitment to the justice and love offered to humanity by a Crucified God. In the barrio, Salvadorans wisely argue that the problem with mainline American Methodism is that too many congregations are caught up in a church-growth logic that prevents them from fully hearing the gospel and which keeps their members engrossed in a material and conformist dominant culture. They note that too many dominant-culture churches avoid being good news to those who feel unwanted and unloved. For Salvadorans who are helping to plant a new church of the poor in the barrio, the church should not reflect the power schemes or prejudices of the surrounding society, but represent an alternative to them in light of the gospel.

Although a subdivision of American Methodists have joined in solidarity with the poor in various parts of the world, very little

---

10. Ethnographic interview with Ramiro, January 1992.

connection is made with the ongoing passion of Christ in the barrio. American Methodists are drawn to the world of the poor mostly in Africa, out of a sense of compassion for human beings; yet, too many have closed themselves off from God calling them to the side of the hungry, unloved, homeless, disinherited, imprisoned, exiled, sick, and destitute of the nation's Latino/a neighborhoods. Mainline Christians, then, are failing to discover in the barrio something fundamental about God, a context of truth and a way to follow Jesus in the world that seeks the kingdom through acts of justice and mercy. The plain God-talk of people in the barrio recognizes that God descends into the world in the condition of poverty and calls the church to hear from this world the demands of the gospel.

I think the new barrio church of the poor promises to reshape the Christian identity of Methodist congregations. By taking seriously the contributions of the barrio to Christian life, church leaders will learn to reaffirm the transforming dimensions of the gospel, move toward a new understanding of the nature of the church, and be liberated from a numbing status quo. American Methodism is invited to the barrio to reclaim its Christian identity at the margins of society. This means cultivating an understanding of Methodist self-identity that willingly proclaims justice and liberation with the condemned of history. American Methodism will learn to reread the Wesleyan tradition with more radical lenses once its relationship with the poor of the barrio helps expose the epistemological limitation and current practical shortcomings that come from identification with North Atlantic capitalist culture.

Voices from the Margin

You will discover in the barrio that Salvadoran newcomers to the Methodist church first named their experience of God in largely authoritarian regimes characterized by injustice and violence. In the small Christian community that I served in the nation's capital, Salvadoran women particularly talked of their lives under a Salvadoran military regime that allowed soldiers and paramilitary forces to use violence and deadly force to repress religious leaders and their allies in civil society. They remember the repression and slaughter of those who belonged to base Christian communities where they regularly discussed scripture as revelation about God's justice and call to responsible action in the world.[11] They experienced mounting repression, witnessed massacres, listened to wailing mothers of the tortured and disappeared, and converted Archbishop Romero in their native land.

For Salvadorans whose faith was born in the daily struggle for human rights, there is no debating that women were the first followers of Jesus and the original witnesses to his resurrection. They believe Jesus rejected the patriarchal society of his day that made women inferior in all things. Salvadoran women in particular do not need seminary training to sensitize them theologically to the way Jesus opposed the male oppressive and discriminatory tradition that kept women from studying and commenting on the Torah, praying, teaching, or bearing witness in court. For Marisol, who associated with the Methodist charge I served as pastor in Washington, D.C., the Bible helps interpret daily life.[12] Marisol was a catechist who led Bible study in El Salvador, a practice she continues now as a stranger in the new land of the barrio. She remembers the way her priest, the late Ignacio Martin-Baro, S. J., made Scripture come alive:

> I attended the Catholic church in El Salvador, the base Christian community church. I was a catechist. The Jesuit Father Ignacio Martin-Baro and Fabian Amaya were our priests. When I went to mass I felt that the priests' sermons were not the same as other priests I experienced in the church. The others talked about the spirit, God, and the importance of constant prayer, but everything was very spiritualized in the style of what we call, alleluia! The spirituality was celestially centered as if the angels were going to come down and carry you off with your shoes. Father

11. Salvadoran women who gathered in small groups in El Salvador to study Scripture and reflect on local, national, and international issues continue the practice in the context and culture of U. S. barrios.

12. In the eighth chapter of *Mujerista Theology* (Maryknoll: Orbis Books, 1996), Ada María Isasi-Díaz observes that for the majority of Hispanic women the Bible is not the starting point for doing theology; instead, the theological point of departure for them is experience and struggle for survival. I found that for Latina newcomers to the barrio who arrive with backgrounds in the base Christian community and who were shaped by grassroots popular culture, liberative reading of the Scriptures is central to their identity. For these Central American women, the Bible is a cultural resource for shaping the political identity of struggle on women's issues as well as for determining views on the justice issues of Latino/a marginality.

Ignacio Martin-Baro, Father Nacho as we called him, was very understandable when he preached, he talked about social reality, real situations. There was dialogue and sharing, the whole community discussed the biblical text and meaning of the gospel that was read. I came to understand that Jesus did not come to start a religion, but to reveal God. Faith that favors the oppressed as it states in the beatitudes fulfills the will of God.[13]

Because male voices and leadership have traditionally been privileged in church and society, Latinas were systematically excluded from the production of theological discourse. But today Latinas are actively opposing the structured identity imposed on them by the dominant culture and a male-dominated church, which are characterized by exclusion, opposition, and negation. Like Marisol, Latinas are shaping the barrio church as a privileged locus from which to unfold oppositional narratives with scripture as a cultural resource of individual and communal liberation.[14] Latinas confront male-dominant power structures that deny them worth, by assuming leadership in barrio churches and grassroots human rights organizations, thus creating new conditions for theological reflection.

Like Marisol, Latinas loudly proclaim that Jesus favored the establishment of life together based on freedom, reconciliation, and solidarity. Latinas remind the entire church that Jesus repeatedly treated women with respect and dignity, even pausing to converse with those who were considered heretics, racially inferior and godless prostitutes. Through people like Marisol, Methodist Latinas are more aware that Jesus welcomed rejected women as daughters of God into a new community, which dared break the rules of the dominant male system. As the barrio church of the poor continues to challenge the center with a vision of radical discipleship, Latinas insist that mainstream Christianity live out the liberating message of the gospel by promoting the total liberation of human beings from patriarchal culture.

---

13. Ethnographic interview with Marisol in Washington, D.C., March 1994.

14. The work of Ada María Isasi-Díaz names this liberative praxis *mujerista theology*. This theology privileges Latina experience and struggle as a hermeneutical source that challenges standard understandings of theology, ecclesiology, ethics, political engagement and religious practices. For examination of mujerista theology see Isasi-Díaz, *Mujerista Theology*.

Conclusion

John Wesley realized that the gospel uniquely calls people into a new life together. He found a way to express authentically the gospel in the culture and situations of his time, especially by finding God present in the poor and working classes who yearned for a world not awash in exploitation and injustice. Wesley listened to the needs of those who lived far from centers of power and whose dignity was repeatedly denied by their social conditions. In the setting of marginality, Wesley responded by organizing self-help projects that paved a way for the excluded to experience an empowered way to be in the world. Wesley inspired a radical discipleship in Christian subjects that centered on helping people at the lower rungs of economic and social status discover their liberative capacities.

Contemporary American Methodism has become so focused on the pursuit of institutional stability and cultural privilege that it has lost touch with the very grassroots communities that nourished the evangelical drive of Wesley and the early Methodist movement. Because cultural accommodation is very high on the list of American Methodism's priorities, members of the church are least concerned with affirming the God who unconditionally opts for the poor and crucified. American Methodism has yet to rediscover how in the Crucified Jesus mainline denominations' claim to have correctly defined God is profoundly called into question. Mainstream Methodism will embody a more authentic discipleship once its witness is radicalized by the God of unrestricted Love found in the barrio, who delivers hope and new life to crucified human beings.

John Wesley modeled a radical discipleship that did not hesitate to break bread and act compassionately toward unloved and rejected people in his social context. Today, the radicalizing influence of barrio Christianity offers American Methodism a new lens for remembering the Wesleyan tradition, especially by finding God present in its trampled men, women, and children. Barrio Christians who are carefully rethinking the meaning and the function of discipleship encourage American Methodism to complete what is "lacking in Christ's afflictions" (Col. 1:24 NVI/NIB Biblia

Bilingüe). The rejected people of the barrio call, then, for a radical discipleship that opts for the poor, builds a church that does not separate God from the poor, and promotes activity directed to the restructuring of the social order and dominant culture in the direction of the reign announced by the Crucified Jesus.

CHAPTER 6

HOLINESS AND HEALING

An Asian American Voice Shaping the Methodist Traditions

ANDREW SUNG PARK

Introduction

What I intend to share in this paper is an Asian American perspective on the appropriate direction of twenty-first century Methodism. The Wesleyan Methodist movement emerged from the situations of eighteenth-century England and Europe. Surrounded by the Deism of natural religion, the Lutheranism of *simul justis et peccator* (justified and sinner at the same time), and the increasing influence of deterministic Calvinism, Wesley advocated the importance of heart, appropriating certain aspects of pietism. Against the Lutheran helplessness of our work regarding the doctrine of sanctification, he stressed the importance of our effort to enhance a holy life. Against the latitudinarianism of moral leniency, he emphasized the corruption of human nature in the form of original sin. Against the irresistible grace of Calvinism, Wesley stressed the prevenient grace of God and human freedom.

In such an historic time, it was not an accident that the Methodist movement emphasized sin, repentance, justification, sanctification, and entire sanctification. These themes were vital for the renewal of the church and the society at that time.

Our time is different from the time of eighteenth-century England in terms of social problems. During the 1960s, social consciousness of civil rights and women's rights was raised, and since the 1980s, people have broken their silence as the victims of sin— child abuse, sexual abuse, sexism, racism, and homophobia—as they courageously came out and shared their stories of deep pain in public. Since the 1965 amendment of the 1952 exclusionary McCarran-Walter Immigration and Nationality Act replaced national quotas with hemispheric limitations, the number of Asian immigrants has increased; particularly in 1975, a huge number of Vietnamese made a great exodus into the United States after the fall of Saigon. Since the 1960s, this nation has witnessed the surge of the outcries of the wounded, while Reinhold Niebuhr's theme of "man as sinner" has faded into a back stage. On the one hand, Asian American communities have grappled with their own wounds directly or indirectly inflicted by the Pacific War, the Japanese American internment, the Korean War, and the Vietnam War. On the other hand, they have accumulated additional wounds in this country, wounds caused mainly by racial discrimination and sexism. Along with other oppressed groups, Asian American churches have found the issue of the woundedness of their people to be more pressing than that of their sin.

In this essay, I propose that Methodist churches develop some steps to care for the wounded. This does not mean overlooking the reality of sin, but rather points to the fact that by dealing with the issue of people's wounds, we can see the mode of sin more holistically. As a matter of fact, the Asian mind does not exclude sin from woundedness. The Asian mind operates, not on the basis of "either/or," but on the basis of "both/and."[1] Built on the idea of Tao that is the foundation of the Asian mind, people in Asia embrace yin and yang, passive and active, empty and full, female and male, still and moving, margin and center, and soft and hard, keeping a dynamic balance between them. Inheriting the Asian mind, Asian Americans have the thought pattern of "both/and." This inclusive mind is what Asian American Methodists can contribute

---

1. Jung Yong Lee, *Marginality: The Key to Multicultural Theology* (Minneapolis: Fortress Press, 1995), 64-65.

to the Wesleyan traditions by developing doctrines for both sinners and their victims.

The balance between them, however, does not happen in a relation of simple equality. It does so rather in a relation of dynamic equity. In this dynamic balance, when yin expands, yang recedes; when yang expands, yin retreats. This is the principle of the dynamic balance of complementarity.[2] According to this vision of balance the church needs to treat fairly the issues of the sinner and the sinned-against. To generate the dynamic balance of doctrines for the sinner and the sinned-against, Methodists need to pay more attention to the sinned-against from an Asian American perspective.

Furthermore, while yang, male, active, and hard had been favored over yin, female, passive, and soft in the traditions of Asia, Lao Tzu, the founder of Taoism, reversed the priority by opting for the latter categories.[3] So, Taoism favors yin over yang, female over male, passive over active, and soft over hard.

For over two hundred years, Methodists have emphasized the ideas of sin, repentance, justification (salvation), and sanctification. It is time for Asian American Methodists to develop certain doctrines for the sinned-against—woundedness *(han)*, resistance, justice (liberation), and healing, based on the Asian heritage and Wesleyan tradition. Let us briefly review these notions.

Han *(Woundedness) and Sin*

In the church, we find all kinds of people from all walks of life— sinners, victims, and others. In Christian theology, there is only one category used to diagnose the wrong of the world: sin. We have drawn the map of salvation for sinners and have left out the sinned-against from the blueprint of salvation in our theology. What about the healing of the sinned-against? It is necessary for us to specify the pain of the sinned-against, because naming a problem is the beginning of its solution. In the Korean and Vietnamese languages, the deep wound of victims is called *han*.

---

2. *I Ching*, trans. Richard Wilhelm and Cary F. Baynes, 3rd ed. (Princeton: Princeton University Press, 1967), Chap. 2 *K'un: the Receptive*.

3. A. C. Graham, *Disputers of the Tao: Philosophical Argument in Ancient China* (La Salle: Open Court, 1989), 223-31.

The Definition of *Han*

Han is the abysmal pain that festers in the heart of the broken-hearted. A story can explain its reality best:

> Eddy Wu, a 23-year-old Chinese-American, was carrying groceries to his car when he was attacked on the afternoon of November 8, 1995, in the parking lot of a supermarket in Novato, California, by Robert Page, who stabbed him twice. Chasing Wu into the super market, Page stabbed him two more times. Wu suffered several serious injuries, including a punctured lung. In his confession, Page, an unemployed musician, said: "I didn't have anything to do when I woke up. No friends were around. It seemed that no one wanted to be around me. So I figured, 'What the f— I'm going to kill me a Chinaman.'" He also said he wanted to kill an Asian because they "got all the good jobs." Page pleaded guilty to attempted murder and a hate crime, and was sentenced to eleven years.[4]

To Eddy, the experience was a nightmare. He had done nothing to deserve his suffering; he was attacked only because of his Asian look. Although America is his home, his different appearance causes him to be regarded as a permanent outsider and enemy. The physical and mental wounds Eddy has received cannot be described by any term but *han*.

Besides Eddy Wu and his family, many Asian Americans have developed anger, frustration, and feelings of helplessness after hearing of this heinous and nonsensical crime. Asian Americans have been treated as disloyal, unfit strangers in their homeland. *Han* epitomizes this combination of anger, frustration, helplessness, and permanent homelessness.

Han can be compared to the black hole in astrophysics. A star several times more massive than our sun grows old and expands to become what is called a red giant. As the red giant reaches maximum enlargement, the inner core of the star implodes and its exterior rebounds. The result is known as a supernova. After the explosion, the star collapses into its center—a singularity. This collapsed star is a black hole; its gravity is so strong that even a beam of light cannot escape from it. Whatever it touches, it swallows up.[5]

---

4. Kenneth B. Noble, "Attacks Against Asian-Americans Are Rising," *The Los Angeles Times*, 12 December 1995.

5. Carl Sagan, *Cosmos* (New York: Random House, 1980), 238-42.

Like the black hole, as the suffering of a victim reaches the maximum limit, it implodes and collapses into a compressed core of pain. This collapsed pain is *han*, generated by unjust psychological, physical, social, political, economic, and cultural repression and oppression.[6] It entrenches itself in the soul of the victims of sin and crime, and is manifested in diverse reactions such as those of the survivors of the Nazi holocaust, the Palestinians in the occupied territories, the racially discriminated-against, the molested, the abused, and the exploited.

Sin causes *han* and *han* produces sin. Sin is of oppressors; *han* is of the oppressed. The sin of oppressors may cause a chain reaction by the *han* of the oppressed. Sometimes *han* reproduces *han*. Also, sin and *han* collaborate to engender *han*. They overlap in many tragic areas of life.

If *han* is improperly treated, it takes revenge on the person who created it or on the wrong people. Daughters-in-law who suffered the suppression of their mothers-in-law afflict in turn their own daughters-in-law. Victims of violence often victimize others, continuing the vicious cycle of victimization.

John Wesley stressed the problem of sin, particularly original sin, yet was very concerned about the reality of suffering caused by sinners. He believed that national sins had produced miseries at home and abroad.

> Now, let each of us lay his hand upon his heart, and say, "'Lord, is it I?' Have I added to this flood of unrighteousness and ungodliness, and, thereby, to the misery of my countrymen? Am not I guilty in any of the preceding respects? And do not they suffer, because I have sinned?" If we have any tenderness of heart, any bowels of mercies, any sympathy with the afflicted, let us pursue this thought till we are deeply sensible of our sins, as one great cause of their sufferings.[7]

His rhetorical questions show his understanding of the reality of miseries caused by sins. The misery he refers to is *han*. It is notable that he is sensitive to the wounds of the sinned-against. He clearly cares about their well-being.

---

6. *Han* is a term that Korean minjung (downtrodden) theologians began to employ in the 1970s. See Yong Bock Kim, ed., *Minjung Theology* (Singapore: The Christian Conference of Asia, 1981).

7. Wesley, Sermon 111, "National Sins and Miseries," §II.8, *Works* 3:575.

Furthermore, he urges us to repent of our sins so that the victims of our sins may be alleviated from their suffering. If we are unable to compensate our victims directly, we can help the poor or the exploited instead.

> And "now let my counsel be acceptable to" you, to every one of you present before God. "Break off thy sins by repentance, and thy iniquities by showing mercy to the poor, if it may be a lengthening of thy tranquillity,"—of what degree of it still remains among us.[8]

Wesley mentioned the need for showing mercy to the poor, leaving up to us the task of how to heal the wounds of our victims. In line with Wesley, Methodists must see beyond the issue of sins and systemic sins and must diagnose where pains lie and grapple with the issue of the pains and wounds for the sinned-against in the church, society, and the world. To heal the world, particularly the two-thirds world, it is necessary to analyze the causes of the wounds of peoples, strategize how to break their causes, and work toward their healing. We need to work on these as rigorously as we have analyzed the causes of sin.

Refusal and Repentance

If a minister visits Eddy Wu in the hospital, she or he cannot urge him to repent of his sin. Eddy's issue is not the repentance of his sin but his refusal of a distorted self-image. It is much easier for Eddy to internalize the values of his assailant and the racist social values of the dominant group than to keep his own self-identity. Victims need to be encouraged to reject low self-esteem and hierarchical social values. For victims, repentance is not a virtue but a misplaced doctrine that fosters a distorted self-image and self-hatred.

People usually have the sense of inviolability, invulnerability, and security before they are attacked or violated. After being violated, however, victims lose their sense of inviolability and retreat into deep fear and unhealthy and unreal self-images. To resist distorted self-images, they have to keep nurturing their healthy images.

---

8. Ibid., 452.

This is possible by getting engaged in the transformation of biased social values. Here the internal refusals of victims need to coincide with the social refusals of the system of bias, unjust social values, oppression, exploitation, and dominance.

During Wesley's time, slavery was a pivotal issue. He strongly opposed the institution of slavery, encouraging William Wilberforce to keep up his good work against slavery in Britain: "Unless God has raised you up for this very thing, you will be worn out by the opposition of men and devils. . . . O be not weary of well doing! Go on, in the name of God and in the power of his might, till even American slavery (the vilest that ever saw the sun) shall vanish away before it."[9] Wesley's heart burned with the sense of the justice of God, denouncing social evils and particularly slavery.

Needless to say, as he encouraged Wilberforce, so would Wesley encourage American slaves to reject the slavery system rather than be subject to it and repent of their sins. The Bible is full of stories of refusal against injustice and evil: the Exodus, Esther, Peter and John under arrest (Acts 4), and the heroes and heroines of faith (Heb. 11). If we are alive, we must resist evil with good, injustice with justice, and untruth with truth. This world is absurd and insane. Refusal of the world is a sign of sanity in the world (Camus). Only dead fish go along with the stream, but live ones swim against it.

It is time for Methodists to build the practice of personal and communal refusal of injustice and abuses for the sinned-against, on the basis of both a biblical and theological doctrine, and the development of the idea of repentance for the sinner. In accordance with Wesley's spirit, Methodists should play the vital role of initiating a doctrine of resistance against many forms of personal, social, and global oppression.

Justice and Justification

To the Roman Catholic Church, justification by faith implies that we actually become righteous by God's grace, mainly by means of

---

9. Letter to William Wilberforce (24 February 1791), *Letters* (Telford) 8:265.

the sacraments. Not by faith alone, but by faith informed by love are we justified. God's grace makes us virtually righteous. The Reformers stressed that by faith alone we are justified through God's grace. God's grace imputes righteousness to us. The Reformation took place when Luther realized that we are justified by faith alone *(sola fide)*. He believed that sinners cannot do anything to earn God's salvation, but receive salvation through God's grace alone. Calvin continued that tradition by emphasizing the irresistible nature of God's saving grace. His understanding of divine grace allows no place for human involvement in the process of justification.

Wesley accepted the significance of faith in our salvation, but went beyond the forensic dimension of justification, extending it to holiness of life and saying:

> Though it be allowed, that both this repentance and its fruits are necessary to full salvation, yet they are not necessary either in the *same sense* with faith, or in the *same degree*. Not in the same degree; for these fruits are only necessary *conditionally,* if there be time and opportunity for them. Otherwise a man may be sanctified without them. But he cannot be sanctified without faith.[10]

Wesley did not neglect the fruition of repentance, which might be interpreted as works by the Reformers. While the Reformers focused on our imputed righteousness by justification by faith, Wesley highlighted actual holiness by faith, not separating justification from its fruition in sanctification. His holiness involves social relatedness, not personal isolation from the world. In this social religion, both the sinner and the sinned-against need to get involved in transforming the world:

> I shall endeavor to show that Christianity is essentially a social religion, and that to turn it into a solitary religion is indeed to destroy it. By Christianity I mean that method of worshipping God which is here revealed to man by Jesus Christ. When I say this is essentially a social religion, I mean not only that it cannot subsist so well, but that it cannot subsist at all, without society, without living and conversing with other men.[11]

---

10. Sermon 43, "The Scripture Way of Salvation," §III.13, *Works* 2:167.
11. Sermon 24, "Upon Our Lord's Sermon on the Mount, IV," §I.1, *Works* 1:533-34.

Wesley understood the importance of the relational aspects of justification. For Wesley, sinners cannot be justified by themselves if they have the opportunity to bear the fruits of repentance. In their relationships with the sinned-against, they can bear the fruits of repentance.

For the sinned-against, justice is an important issue. To Eddy Wu, restoring justice is a more pressing matter than imputed righteousness. Wesley was aware of the significance of ministry for justice and emphasized the task of caring for the wounded and their rights:

> First, "how beautiful are the feet" of those who are sent by the wise and gracious providence of God to execute justice on earth, to defend the injured, and punish the wrongdoer! Are they not "the ministers of God to us for good," the grand supporters of the public tranquillity, the patrons of innocence and virtue, the great security of all our temporal blessings?[12]

For Wesley, the beauty of ministry is to advocate for the wounded and to restore justice. Methodists need to focus on the ministry of justice in addition to the ministry of the justification of the sinner by faith. The wounded also should work on reinstating their own rights. They cannot depend on others' work for attaining their own rights; they should labor for rectifying injustice. This work of the restoration of justice is the expression of faith for both the sinned-against and sinners.

Faith is trusting in God's mercy (Luther), but who has faith makes a difference in defining its specific meaning. When we read the Bible, we see faith manifested in at least two different ways: the faith of sinners and the faith of the sinned-against. The faith of sinners relies on God's mercy, while the faith of the sinned-against trusts in the fairness of God. If sinners have faith in God, they will be *justified by God*. If the sinned-against have faith in God, they will count on the *justice of God*. The faith of sinners denotes the reliance upon *divine acceptance and validation,* while the faith of the sinned-against trusts in *divine judgment and vindication.* Since we have treated the faith of sinners exclusively, let us give attention to the faith of the sinned-against.

---

12. Sermon 15, "The Great Assize," §IV.1, *Works* 1:371.

The phrase *the faith of the just* appears in Habbakuk. In the book of Habbakuk, faith meant waiting. Habbakuk lived in the time when evil people prospered. His main complaint was why a just God is "silent when the wicked swallow those more righteous than they" (1:13). At his watchtower, he kept watch to see what God would say to him. Finally God answered him and said: "Write the vision; make it plain on tablets, so that a runner may read it. For there is still a vision for the appointed time; it speaks of the end, and does not lie. If it seems to tarry, wait for it; it will surely come, it will not delay. Look at the proud! Their spirit is not right in them, but *the righteous live by their faith*" (2:2-4).[13] Faith is an unswerving *waiting* for God's verdict upon the wicked. *Waiting* signifies trusting in God's fair ruling for everyone. For sinners, faith means trusting in God's pardoning grace that *makes* them righteous (Roman Catholics) or *regards* them as righteous (Protestants). For the sinned-against, faith denotes trusting in God's grace that reinstates God's *justice* by restoring their *rights*—human rights and civil rights. For Habbakuk, faith is waiting for God's vindication of the wronged. Trusting in the faithfulness of God for the restoration of justice is the gist of the book of Habbakuk.

In the New Testament, Jesus was the ultimate norm of faith—"the pioneer and perfecter of our faith, who for the sake of the joy that was set before him endured the cross" (Heb. 12:2). By faith Jesus endured the cross, not for the sake of his own justification but for the sake of others. Who are the "others"? They are the persecuted or the sinned-against: "Consider him who endured such hostility against himself from sinners, so that you may not grow weary or lose heart" (Heb. 12:3). The faith of the persecuted comes from Christ, who provides them the courage to trust in God's justice. Jesus sought not the justification of the persecuted, but their strength of trust in God to endure oppression and overcome it.

Healing and Holiness

Victims are primarily concerned with the healing of their *han*, not with holiness. For Eddy Wu, physical and mental healing are more urgent matters to attend to than the matter of his own sanctification.

---

13. Emphasis mine.

No one, however, can find the source of healing within oneself. Healing takes place in God's grace, which makes one whole. Wholeness is the natural consequence of deepening the spiritual fellowship with God. Healing is wholeness.

In the Hebrew Bible, wholeness is expressed in the term *shalom* (*šālôm*). This is also the principal word used to express the idea of peace in Hebrew. Among its root words within Semitic languages, the Akkadian *salāmū*, comes nearest to the essential meaning of the root, "to be whole, complete." Representing the notions of wholeness, health, and completeness, *shalom* not only points to the absence of war in a purely negative sense, but also involves friendship between two peoples (see Judg. 4:17; Isa. 7:14; 1 Kgs. 5:4, 26; 22:45).[14]

Furthermore, healing is more than just restoring what was hurt, but also enlarging one's own wholeness beyond the healing of his or her wound by laying a new starting point for the transformation of social structures that cause *han*. Eddy's healing cannot occur at an individual level alone; it has structural dimensions. The xenophobia and racism that caused his *han* must be dismantled. Since Eddy's wholeness is closely related to societal wholeness, his healing will grow beyond the individual level.

Wesley stressed healing through grace too. In his sermon "Upon Our Lord's Sermon on the Mount, VI" he discussed healing, using his poem "A Paraphrase on the Lord's Prayer":

> Spirit of grace, and health, and power,
> Fountain of light and love below;
> Abroad thine healing influence shower,
> O'er all the nations let it flow.
> Inflame our hearts with perfect love.[15]

Wesley pays tribute to the Spirit of grace that administers healing, welling up light and love. To him, grace's purpose is not only to justify the sinner, but also to heal the wounded. Wesley is definitely concerned about the marginalized and the oppressed in his scheme of salvation by pointing out that God's grace heals the

---

14. Joseph P. Healey, "Peace: the Old Testament," in *The Anchor Bible Dictionary*, ed. David Noel Freedman (New York: Doubleday 1992), 5:206-7. See also R. de Vaux, *Ancient Israel: Its Life and Institutions*, trans. J. McHugh (New York: McGraw Hill, 1965), 254.

15. Sermon 26, "Sermon on the Mount, VI," *Works* 1:590.

wounds of the marginalized while justifying and sanctifying the sinner.

He further urges us to cooperate with God's healing. God's grace works through us: "Heal the sick; not by miracle, but through the blessing of God upon your seasonable support. Let the blessing of him that was ready to perish through pining want come upon thee. Defend the oppressed, plead the cause of the fatherless, and make the widow's heart sing for joy."[16]

Wesley instructs all of us to get involved in healing the wounded, uplifting the downtrodden, and protecting the defenseless. He wants us to be part of God's grace that restores wounded parties to health and wholeness. God's grace employs us as miracle workers, instead of making us dependent on God's intervention.

God achieves the healing of the sinned-against and the sanctification of the sinner in the process of synergetic healing. By setting the wounded free from their oppression, the Spirit heals their wounds. While sanctifying grace makes the justified holy by promoting the fruition of the justified after being justified, healing grace touches the wounded to transcend their sorrows and affects them to keep broadening their healing circles. Graced by the Holy Spirit, the wounded can confront and transform the *han* of the world with their own wounds.

Conclusion

Drawing upon the Tao principles of "both/and" and the dynamic balance of complementarity, the Asian mind embraces center and margin, yin and yang, female and male, the weak and the strong, and the sinned-against and the sinner, particularly advocating the former in each pair. Having the heritage of the Bible, the Asian mind, and the Wesleyan tradition, Asian American Methodists can see the need for the development of certain doctrines for the sinned-against without neglecting doctrines for the sinner: woundedness *(han)*, resistance, justice (liberation), and healing. It is time for all Methodists to pursue the development of these doctrines in the structural transformation of the personal, communal, and social levels of life.

---

16. Sermon 28, "Sermon on the Mount, VIII," §27, *Works* 1:630.

CHAPTER 7

HEARING, HOLINESS, AND HAPPINESS

Listening to God and Neighbor

REBECCA S. CHOPP

After reading the essays in this volume, I—a white middle-class feminist Christian involved in the church of the center—ask myself: How will the church be able to hear the voices on the margins? This book argues the importance of marginalized persons' speaking. But the capacity of the largely white, mainline, middle-class church, hereafter referred to as the center church, to hear these voices is a difficult issue. Being in the center makes it difficult to hear the voices on the margins because the center is supported and secured through the economic, structural, and psycho-socio-linguistic location of precisely those groups of persons on the margins of society. Though "hearing" must be considered as the preliminary step to the center church addressing issues of oppression and injustice, if any work for social transformation by the center church is to occur, then hearing the voices on the margin is a necessary, though not a sufficient, step. If the center church cannot hear the Word of God in the voices of the margins, the faithful action of the center church may be reduced to occasional mission trips or paternalistic gestures of charity. Hearing the Word of God, scripturally and theologically, is the necessary precondition for the right relation with God and neighbor that addresses oppression and injustice.

As a Christian feminist, I have been part of the thirty-five-year feminist movement in the church to beg, convince, and demand that the center church hear the women who have been, in a sense, part of the center, even as they have been on the margins in terms of positions of authority. The ability of the center church to hear the feminist movement in its midst arose from a combination of broad social changes, which forced the church to reevaluate its traditional position on women's roles, and the intimate involvement between women and men as fathers and daughters, mothers and sons, sisters and brothers, and frequently as husbands and wives.[1] The power of feminist advocacy has been greatly enhanced by the personal and social access women have to men who guard the center. Other marginalized groups have not "enjoyed" the same opportunities as have white middle-class women in terms of convincing the center church to enlarge and transform its center. Race in America continues to divide our nation, and the church continues to be one of the most segregated institutions in America. The poor here and in other cultures lack the access to get their voices heard without someone who will help make this happen. And women of all races, classes, and countries are far too often ignored, as the center church subsumes all women under a white feminist perspective.

I want to explore how the white feminist movement in The United Methodist Church can help the center church listen to those on the margin. Feminists have long understood the importance of listening in the life of faith; indeed, the central act of the feminist movement can be described, in the words of Nelle Morton, as "hearing one another into speech."[2] Listening to God as an act of faith, for feminists, has followed the prophetic mandate of hearing God speak against the social mores of the day. And hearing God's truth in the midst of our lives requires, as Jesus suggested, a certain kind of "ears." To not hear God is to be out of relation; and so hearing God, from a feminist perspective, is a fundamental aspect of

---

1. For an analysis of the various social forces, including the popularity of birth control, economic forces requiring middle-class women to work, and changing family structures, that contributed to the "success" of the feminist movement in the church, see my *Saving Work: Feminist Practices of Theological Education* (Louisville: Westminster John Knox, 1995), 23-26.

2. Nelle Morton, *The Journey Is Home* (Boston: Beacon Press, 1985), 55.

staying in right relation to God. Or, to say it a bit differently, the incapacity to hear God in the midst of the world is a sign and act of sin.

Through the process of hearing one another into speech, the feminist movement, in the center church, has helped to move women from margin to center in positions of authority as well as in positions of service. Thirty years ago, white feminist Christians understood women to belong on the margins of the church. Here, the language of margin and center, when applied to the role of white women in the mainline church, has a double meaning. White women have populated the pews and performed the domestic work of the church far more than have white men. Since one definition of the term "margin" is that which supports and provides for the dominant position, women have been the ever-necessary margin as they have provided the bodies in the pews and the domestic workers in the care of the community and outreach of the church. But women have also been on the margin, in the sense that "margin" means that which is excluded from the center; women have not been allowed to be in the authoritative positions of church polity, practice, or thought. As a result of both the feminist movement and the changed reality of women's roles in society, women have moved more into the center of the church. Women have assumed new ordained and lay leadership roles, have added feminist images of God (mother, friend, compassionate one) to the language of faith, have uncovered women's voices in Scripture and in church history, and have encouraged new ways of thinking about church as a community of friends and a countercommunity of justice. Women have created new theologies, new liturgies, and new forms of communal practices for life together in the church. And through their advocacy as well as through their creative interpretation of Christianity, women and men have formed a vital and large feminist movement that continues today in the center church.

The feminist movement, like many social reform movements, is loosely organized and operates at various levels and in various ways within the center church. The movement has garnered great support among women and men mainliners and has produced literature, rituals, conferences, journals, and so on. The movement has been marshaled to elect women as bishops, to pass legislation at General Conference on topics of special concern to women, and to increase the number of women faculty in seminaries and women ministers in annual conferences. The contemporary Christian feminist movement appears to be one of the few spaces and networks to work for transformation within the center church. I certainly do not want to overstate the success of white women in the center of ecclesial structures of power. I only want to describe the fact that white feminists today find themselves more in the center of the church than in former times. And I want to urge feminists, both women and men, to use this location, however fragile and tentative, to shape the church to hear those on the margins as a necessary, but not sufficient, condition for working for justice.

Acknowledging partial transformation of the center by the entrance especially of white women feminists in the UMC must go along with the recognition that the center church is being transformed by a changing American culture. Mainline denominations, such as the United Methodist, are losing members and experiencing significant change in the role of their members. A highly transient population in the U.S. selects churches for personal fit to lifestyles, class locations, and ideological preferences. Gone are the days when the denominations conferred identity upon individuals and persons sought out the same denomination no matter where they moved in the country. Further, as Americans become increasingly suspicious of large bureaucracies, the UMC hierarchy is losing its political and structural influence with individuals and with other institutions. Finally, the parish, with its special signature programs aimed at a particular class and lifestyle, has become the important location of church in American culture. Thus, as many sociologists of religion note, the American church is undergoing radical transformation.[3] But, times of liminality can provide an opportunity to be closed or open to new voices. Feminists in the United Methodist Church now have a powerful opportunity to seize this moment to transform the center church to a church that can hear the voices on the margins.

In this essay, I am going to assume a fundamental acquaintance with feminist theology and with the feminist movements within mainline Christianity. I believe that the feminist movement has a great affinity with Wesley's theology. Feminists view Christianity

---

3. Robert Wuthnow, *Christianity in the 21st Century: Reflections on the Challenges Ahead* (New York: Oxford, 1993).

as a way of love that offers and results in emancipatory transformation.[4] We envision the church as communities in which persons experience the truth of their lives and are formed for the life of love in the world; and we provide a countercultural vision of personal experience. As Wesley offered a radical alternative to the cultural Christianity of his day, so does feminism present a quite different vision of being Christian than the one predominantly offered in the white mainline church today. My perspective, within the confines of this essay, seeks to identify the resources in Wesley's theology that the feminist movement can use to move the church to the active listening of love.

What Is Christianity?

For many persons in our culture, Christianity is a commodity designed to make them feel "spiritual" as one chapter in their story of personal success and fulfillment. The church, somewhat like the car you own or where you live, becomes a provider of individual identity under the guise of constructing "my personal faith story." Religion is dominated by a logic of commodification, and Christians shop for churches as they do for cars, sneakers, and signature clothing. Saturated with media images of happiness and steeped in materialism, contemporary cultural Christians use the narcotic effects of feel-good religion to numb the radicalism of Scripture, tradition, and practices of the church. Moreover, the scriptural, historical, and theological illiteracy of most Christians allows spirituality to be privatized. The inability of denominations to maintain the theological richness of their traditions also allows local churches to define "religious markets" by age, class, and ideological preference. As a seeming matter of survival, mainline churches have done a great deal to accommodate this form of cultural Christianity by providing "customer-friendly" services for individuals, taking care to rearrange church schedules to accommodate the busy lives of families whose individual members engage in so many other important activities.

---

4. For the notion of emancipatory transformation in feminist theology, see my *The Power to Speak: Feminism, Language, God* (New York: Crossroad, 1989), and Elizabeth A. Johnson, *She Who Is: The Mystery of God in Feminist Theological Discourse* (New York: Crossroad, 1992).

If the center church is ever going to hear the margins, it will have to be transformed from this market-driven form of cultural Christianity into a radical way of Christianity. A Wesleyan feminist theology can offer a way of Christianity by combining the feminist insistence on Christian praxis of emancipatory transformation with Wesley's notion of Christianity as a way of love of God and neighbor. Three characteristics of Wesley's notion are worth retrieving in the feminist movement: (1) Christianity is about a way of living in relation to God and neighbor; (2) this way of life is a love of God and neighbor that is described as holiness; and (3) the life of holiness is lived through the means of grace in works of mercy and works of piety.

Christianity, for Wesley, is not about belief, feeling good, or representing one's status in the community. Against the staid orthodoxy of his day, Wesley offered a radical vision of Christianity as a focused, intense way of life that lives in and through relation with God and neighbor in the world. As Theodore Runyon has observed, "Faith is neither subjectivist emotion or rationalist assent operating within the individual, but it is a relation into which we are taken by grace."[5] For Wesley, Christianity was what Albert Outler has called "a life process—which is to say, for Wesley, 'holy living' springing from love of God and neighbor."[6] Wesley and feminists share this view: Christianity orients our whole life and is as much about how we act outside the walls of the church as inside those walls. This claim is about the nature of God in the world; but it is also a claim about the very nature of salvation.

Wesley is a theologian of love: God loves the world and brings us into participation with that love. Our relation to the world becomes an habituation of how we love God and neighbor, with the neighbor being not only the one next door, but the one in need, the one who has injured us, the others of creation. Holiness is the living of this way of love in which we participate and through which we grow. A word that needs to be adopted and adapted for use in feminist theology, "holiness" is the Christian participation in God's love in the world, a love that transforms the brokenness of the world into the new creation even as it transforms the broken-

---

5. Theodore Runyon, *The New Creation: John Wesley's Theology Today* (Nashville: Abingdon Press, 1998), 54.

6. Albert C. Outler, "John Wesley: Folk-Theologian," *Theology Today* 43 (July 1977): 156.

ness of the individual life into a life lived in love with God and neighbor. Holiness is, to use feminist biblical language, our friendship with the world, our "hearing others into speech."

For Wesley, the Christian encountered God through the means of grace: outward signs, appointed by God, for the experience of grace. Given Wesley's stress on Christianity as a way of salvation, the means of grace include active engagement in the world. As Joerg Rieger has pointed out, Wesley expanded the grace tradition by adding works of mercy to the ordinary means of grace in the sacraments and in reading Scripture.[7] In his sermon "On Zeal," Wesley indicates that the works of mercy "are to be preferred." Wesley mandates that even acts of piety such as prayer and fasting should not interfere with responding to the needs of our neighbors. Lest some think Wesley's stress on works of mercy is just a random rhetorical flourish in a sermon, remember that throughout Wesley's ministry, he enacted works of mercy without ceasing.[8] Another way to underscore Wesley's insistence that Christianity is a way of salvation lies in Wesley's emphasis upon the role of good works as not only flowing from faith but also serving to increase it. As Manfred Marquardt notes, "To avoid forfeiting one's faith, then, the believer should be careful not to ignore opportunities to do good, but to strengthen faith by employing it in good works."[9]

This perspective is as radical in our times as it was in Wesley's. In a day when the norm for individual success is fashioned through consumption and the identity of the marketplace, the feminist movement in the church must offer a radical vision of Christianity as a holy way of life of love for God and neighbor. Just as the feminist movement has offered a fundamental revision of Christianity in terms of the images of men and women, as well as a vision of Christianity as a praxis of emancipatory transformation rather than just a system of personal beliefs, it can offer a fundamental revision of Christianity in terms of love of God and neighbor and, in this context, a life of actively hearing others into speech.

---

7. Joerg Rieger, "The Means of Grace, John Wesley, and the Theological Dilemma of the Church Today," *Quarterly Review* 17 (1997): 380.

8. Ibid., 388-89.

9. Manfred Marquardt, *John Wesley's Social Ethics*, trans. John E. Steely and W. Stephen Gunter (Nashville: Abingdon Press, 1992), 99.

A New Vision of Church

If Christianity is a way, rather than a mode, of belief, it is an active hearing of God in the world. But how do we know how to do this? Living a life of faith in the world is complicated, and there is no easy Wesleyan instruction manual to do this. If we want to actively hear God's love in the world, we must be formed and shaped to do so. Comparing this formation to playing music, our ability to follow the music is increased with practice and training to actively hear the music as well as to follow the techniques of playing the instrument itself. Wesley believed that only those who live in holiness are real members of the church. By this Wesley did not mean the sectarian notion that only the pure are in the church, but that those who live following Christ's way, who are engaged in the process of holiness, form the church.

White feminists have written a great deal about the nature of the church or, more formally, ecclesiology. Traditionally, the word "church" has suggested to many persons the hierarchy of priests, the minister in the pulpit, or the church council conducting its solemn business. Theological questions about the church have often revolved about the office of Christ and the office of the clergy, or about how the mission of the church should proclaim or speak the gospel out into the world. Perhaps because feminism draws together the tools of feminist theory with the experience of women performing the "domestic work" of the church, feminist images of church have been based on women finding their friendship in quilting circles and prayer groups, on women organizing endlessly and quietly to provide hospitality to those in need and those new in town, and to offer a different sphere of imagining life together. Feminist ecclesiology has drawn upon the experience of women in the church to image the church, to use the language of Letty Russell, as round table connection, kitchen table solidarity, and welcome table partnership.[10]

One of the UMC churches I served as a pastor provides an insight of how feminist theology shapes its ecclesiology out of the lives of women in the church, women who are both marginal and central to the church. The women in this church functioned as a well-

---

10. Letty M. Russell, *Household of Freedom: Authority in Feminist Theology* (Philadelphia: Westminster Press, 1987).

organized social service network in the community. When a death occurred, the women knew immediately who would bake the necessary cakes and casseroles, who would organize the delivery of the food, and who would be assigned to serve at the dinner. The women were skilled in their ministry: They knew how to do this with support through works and gestures of mercy. A church session might struggle to make a decision to support a petition to an annual conference, but the women's group could perform the complexities of providing food for hundreds of persons without a ripple on the ethos of bereavement. As growing numbers of women work outside the home, this ecclesial work of mercy is more and more difficult to accomplish. There are restaurants and caterers that easily provide this, and families who can afford to purchase this "service." But this work of mercy provides resources for theological reflection on a feminist Wesleyan image of church. Feminist theology has retrieved and refashioned these kinds of women practices of faith for the church of women and men.[11]

Theologians talk of practices today, practices that shape and form persons in the faith. Though Wesley did not employ the language of practices, he certainly understood the insight that individual Christians are formed through communal practices. His bands and classes formed and shaped persons through piety and education but also through practices of mercy. Both feminists and Wesley stress a virtue ethics: Being shaped through engaged and embodied practices, the person and the community are transformed into agents of love. A simple example: Hospitality is a virtue trained and honed by women as they reach out to the families of those who have died, as they provide the service, as they pray together in this work. As they practice hospitality, their capacity to experience God in this way of love grows.

Wesley's notion of holiness assumed, as Theodore Jennings has phrased it, "the capacitation for holiness."[12] Grace really changes persons, and it changes them as they engage in God's work of love in the world. To be capacitated, persons engage in Christian practices of visiting the sick, taking care of the poor, going to prisons. This capacity to participate in grace is Christian love, and it is an

---

11. For an elaboration of how feminist theology shapes practices, see my *Saving Work*.
12. Theodore W. Jennings Jr., *Good News to the Poor: John Wesley's Evangelical Economics* (Nashville: Abingdon Press, 1990), 140.

active love that listens to God in the world. Christian community forms and shapes us in the activity of love both within the community and as the community lives out love in the world.

The feminist movement is actively reshaping the church through practices that stress solidarity, justice, partnership, and hospitality. As Beverly Harrison maintains, we must create moral base-points, or virtues, out of the powerful, nurturing reality of love that allows us to "act-each-other-into-well-being."[13] Wesley's emphasis on works of mercy and piety that build up the holiness of the individual along with the vitality of the church provides important theological resources for feminists as they seek to make the church of the center one that can actively hear God and neighbor in the world. Contemporary feminists must help the church hear God and neighbor in order to begin to address the enormous structural injustice between the rich and poor, and must combine works of mercy with critical analysis of systems of oppressions and destruction. Wesley failed to offer any kind of systematic analysis of poverty and oppression, but he does provide resources for us to shape a church that can begin to hear the need for such analysis and, in this fashion, to hear God and those neighbors on the margins.

A Christian Attitude of Delight

In reading Wesley, I am always struck by his insistence on the Christian way as a way of happiness and delight in God. For many years, I have tended to brush this off as romanticism or sweet piety. But, as I witness more and more the demonic power of materialism and commodification of individuals within our social system, I wonder if part of Wesley's radicalism for our day and age is the claim that the Christian way is a life of happiness and delight in God. That is to say, for the center church to hear those on the margins, the fundamental psycho-socio-spiritual construct of the self must change from the commodification of desire to a construct of joy and delight in God. So long as individuals construct and experience "life" through acquisition of material goods, any listening to

13. Beverly Wildung Harrison, "The Power of Anger in the Work of Love: Christian Ethics for Women and Other Strangers," in *Making the Connections: Essays in Feminist Social Ethics,* ed. Carol S. Robb (Boston: Beacon Press, 1985), 11.

God and the margins will function as a bandage over spiritual wounds that such commodification keeps raw or as a release valve for the exhaust from such consumption. I am convinced not only that our economic and political structures need to change, but also that our emotional, psychological, and spiritual constructs, or what can be called our socio-symbolic order, must change.[14] Wesley is especially helpful on the latter change, which he anticipates the eschatological transformation will create: "Hence will arise an unmixed state of holiness and happiness far superior to that which Adam enjoyed in paradise."[15] Note the emphasis not only on holiness, as love of God and neighbor, but also on the state of happiness. And Wesley is quite clear that the attempt to satisfy human desire in worldly goods is not the Christian way:

> The seeking of happiness in what gratifies either the desire of the flesh, by agreeably striking upon the outward senses; the desire of the eye, of the imagination, by its novelty, greatness, or beauty; or the pride of life, whether by pomp, grandeur, power, or the usual consequence of them, applause and admiration: "is not of the Father"—cometh not from, neither is approved by, the Father of spirits—"but of the world"—it is the distinguishing mark of those who will not have [God] reign over them.[16]

Perhaps from the margin, this emphasis on the relation of spiritual happiness to holiness sounds narcissistic and numbing. But I think Wesley, who argued this strongly in his day, understood the gospel's power to work against the most damning economic, psychological, and social structures of his time. The Christian way is not the way of the world; its antidote to the power of commodification is a strong one that says real happiness exists with participation in God's delight in the world. Until Christians in the center church begin to live this holiness and happiness, they will not experience the power of this delight and this saving grace. Wesley understood the gospel and he understood its power to make persons hear. "This repentance, this faith, this peace, joy, love; this

---

14. For a feminist analysis of the need for political, social, and personal change, see Chopp, *The Power to Speak*.

15. Sermon 64, "The New Creation," §18, *Works* 2:510.

16. Sermon 17, "The Circumcision of the Heart," §I.13, *Works* 1:409.

change from glory to glory, is what the wisdom of the world has voted to be madness, mere enthusiasm, utter distraction."[17]

Feminism has struggled to find its own fundamental resistance to a similar dominant psycho-socio-linguistic formation. For feminism, what it is to be a woman had to be resisted in small ways and in large ones. Though women are "climbing the ladder," there is still enormous struggle on an individual level to find a way of wholeness in a culture that now says woman must be helpmate and breadwinner, sex symbol and CEO, mother and full-time employee. Through feminist theology, literature, arts, and countless other ways, women are seeking to define a way of meaningful existence that is different from that of the dominant order. As the feminist movement has led the church in resisting the dominant subject position of women as defined only through helpmate and sex object, so also should feminism lead the church in forming and shaping Christian attitudes of delight in the other, of joy in listening, of happiness that comes with the capacitation for holiness. Until the psycho-socio-linguistic position of Christians in the center is transformed, I do not believe they can hear those on the margins.

Conclusion

Some may believe that those who live in the center of American culture—steeped in materialism, overly busy with career and family demands, saturated with media images and promises of quick fulfillment, hungry for speedy spiritual highs—are beyond the power of hearing. But my own Wesleyan theology tells me that God is everywhere: in the lives of the rich and poor, women and men, or, in the terms of this book, the margin and center. The opportunity for Christian feminism is to shape the center church to hear by offering a radical vision of Christianity, creating communities of practices that form persons and church into holiness and providing a construct of the self that loves God and neighbor. I want to end the essay by stating again that shaping the center church to hear does not replace the priority of the voices on the margin, nor does it replace the need for a critical analysis of oppres-

---

17. Sermon 7, "The Way to the Kingdom," §II.13, *Works* 1:231.

sive systems. But in the center church where many are numbed by the narcotic effects of cultural Christianity, some attempt to "hear" may be one small, but important and necessary contribution. If those on the margins speak, those in the center need to be able to hear. It is only through hearing the word of God and neighbor that radical transformation, including the emancipatory transformation of changing oppressive social systems and unjust economic systems, occurs. Hearing God's word is a necessary, though not a sufficient, condition for the transformation of the center church so that it may join in solidarity with those on the margins to work for God's restoration of creation and God's radical transformation of the world.

PART III
RADICAL METHODISM IN GLOBAL PERSPECTIVE

CHAPTER 8

THE RADICALISM OF PRIMITIVE METHODISM

STEPHEN G. HATCHER

An essential quality within the ministry of John Wesley was his pragmatism. Wesley shaped Christian teaching according to need and experience. He did not intend that a pattern of interpretation for his own day should fossilize into a "doctrine" for all time. Thus, Wesley's motivation partly was to respond to real need among his contemporaries, and especially among those who needed him most. But paramount was his sense of call, which had "messianic" qualities. The inner conviction was such that response must be made—irrespective of the consequences. This insight into the motivation and significance of John Wesley has been seen as Wesley's "messianic consciousness." It manifested itself in a fivefold "radicalism"—Passion of the Heart, Rising of the Poor, Radical Discipleship, A Church of the People, and Theology from the Bottom.[1]

However, when John Wesley died in 1791 he left no captain on the bridge of the ship called Methodism. Inevitably there were a number of opinions about the future direction of that ship and its ultimate destination.

Some believed that the key issues related to the sacraments and ministry, to the education of converts still raw in the faith, and to

---

1. See John J. Vincent, *OK, Let's Be Methodists* (London: Epworth, 1984).

the relationship of the Methodist people to others. At a time of revolution in Europe and growing distress at home, these Methodists were very conscious of the fact that the establishment, both of state and church, had a wary eye on the Methodist people. In the fullness of time the Methodists who thought like this became the Wesleyan Methodists.

There were other Methodists who yearned for democracy in their church. Wesley had been autocratic in his control, and because he was Wesley, this had been largely accepted. But if lesser "Wesleys" tried the same thing, there would be trouble. In Leeds a new denomination was actually formed by former Wesleyan Methodist members who objected not just to the introduction of an organ, but even more to the behavior of the trustees who had introduced that organ "over the heads of the members and against their wishes." In due course this quest for participatory lay democracy would find its constitutional expression in the various component parts of what in 1907 became the British United Methodist Church.

Those who thought in a third way became the Primitive Methodists. The response of Hugh Bourne, William Clowes, James Steele, and others who joined with them was without compromise. They said in effect: If we are Methodists, we do what Methodists do. Wesley was nothing if he was not a field preacher. Wesley said: Go not just to those who need you, but also to those who need you most. We must do the same. In one sense they ignored the fact that they lived in tumultuous times—because their call was absolute. In another sense, because of their working-class identity they interpreted Wesley for their own age and became extremely effective at winning working-class folk in a way that would leave the other branches of Methodism standing. They would, for instance, develop open-air "field preaching" into the British "camp meeting," and thereby demonstrate that they stood firmly in the line of Wesley's pragmatism. Amidst rapid social change they would shape both method and teaching to a new age.

In the generation from 1807, the people who called themselves Primitive Methodists (but who were nicknamed "Ranters") would thus successfully organize open-air gatherings around the country, to which plain folk would flock by the thousands. When the Ranter preacher tried the same thing on the street or in the marketplace, he was in danger of finishing up in a filthy jail, so most "camp meetings" were held in the countryside. Preachers walked everywhere and built a working-class denomination at a rate that even exceeded the growth of early Methodism under Wesley.[2]

The Primitive Methodist story is sometimes told as if the only issue was the open-air preaching. An American Methodist called Lorenzo Dow had brought news about wonderful events on the frontier as the settlers moved steadily to the west. More good had been done through the camp meetings as a means of grace than through all the other various attempts of organized religion put together. In spite of the weather, the culture, and the wider environment all being quite different in England, Hugh Bourne was persuaded by Dow to have a go. The first English camp meeting was thus held at Mow Cop on the Cheshire-Staffordshire border on May 31, 1807. The fact that approximately two thousand people were present for the day on the bleak hillside at a height of 1,000 feet above sea level, proved the serious intent. Official Wesleyan Methodism dissociated itself entirely from the proceedings, and in due course would expel the leaders from membership of the local Methodist society.

This familiar description of events is satisfactory as far as it goes. What it does not say is that Bourne's camp meetings were a combination of the American experience, Wesley's field preaching, and Bourne's own innovation.[3]

It must also be recognized that there were many facets to the whole character of Primitive Methodism that gave it both a radical and a working-class ethos. The various threads that made up this character will now therefore be investigated.

(1) Bourne and Clowes were of the working classes. While Jabez Bunting, the Wesleyan figure most determined to usher that movement to the right hand of the establishment, looked down on the

---

2. John T. Wilkinson, "The Rise of Other Methodist Traditions," in *A History of the Methodist Church in Great Britain*, ed. R. Davies, A. R. George, G. Rupp (London: Epworth, 1978), 2:276-329; Bourne MS (Auto) A text f19, f121; Hugh Bourne, *History of the Primitive Methodists up to the Year 1823* (Bemersley: J. Bourne, 1823), 4; H. B. Kendall, *The Origin and History of the Primitive Methodist Church* (London: Dalton, 1905), 1:10; Bourne MS Journal (1 April 1803), A f33, 18 Nov 1848, T f25; *Minutes* (British) 28 June 1744, *Minutes* (British) 18 June 1747; *Minutes* (British) 1797, section XII; and Stephen Hatcher, "Hugh Bourne's Debt to John Wesley," *Methodist Recorder* (31 March 1988): 20.

3. *Minutes* (British) 1807, Q21; John C. Bowmer, *Pastor and People* (London: Epworth, 1975), 82; Hugh Bourne, *An Account of a Memorable Camp Meeting that was held by the Methodists on Sunday the 31st May, Mow Cop* (Warrington: J. Haddock, 1807); W. E. Farndale, *The Secret of Mow Cop* (London: Epworth, 1950), 29; William Garner, *Jubilee of English Camp Meetings* (London: T. King, 1857), 52; Lorenzo Dow, *History of Cosmopolite; or the Writings of Rev. Lorenzo Dow*, 8th edition (Cincinnati: Applegate & Co., 1854), 720.

workers from the great height of connectional intrigue, Bourne and Clowes were of the working people.

To read the biography of Bunting beside that of Hugh Bourne, the earnest-millwright and joiner (called in to improvise machinery, repair timbering, or do iron work at collieries or "mountain farms" in Staffordshire) who founded the Primitive Methodists, is to pass between two different worlds. We can scarcely discuss the two churches in the same terms.[4]

Bourne mixed with and worked with the colliers from Kidsgrove and Harriseahead, who lived like lepers outside the camp. They were without education, without health care, without a place of worship or a place of meeting, and it looked very much as if no one cared. But Bourne cared. Of course in many ways his shy, sensitive soul recoiled from them strongly, but his calling was such that he helped a notorious swearer and drunkard called Daniel Shubotham to get religion, and thereby caused a stir that helped launch a revival. Largely at his own expense, Bourne built these noisy expressive colliers a chapel at Harriseahead. It would serve not only for preaching and praying but also for the education of their children in the Sunday school.[5]

(2) Primitive Methodism was highly participatory. The camp meetings developed by Bourne involved a range of different religious exercises with a high level of participation and with a choice for the casual visitor. In four corners of the field four different meetings could take place. Singing, praying, relating experience, and very short preaching would be interspersed. All the time this was happening the "pious praying laborers" would be establishing through their prayers a chain with three links—the hearer, the leader, and the Almighty. A modern parallel can be found in the radio magazine program with a short series of items, and nothing lasting more than two or three minutes. It would also be possible to tune in to another station if the first program did not satisfy. The camp meeting equivalent was to move to a different corner of the field.[6]

4. E. P. Thompson, *The Making of the English Working Class* (Harmondsworth: Penguin Books, 1968), 436.

5. Hugh Bourne, *History*, 9; *Primitive Methodist Magazine* (1836): 178-79; *Notices of the Early Life of Hugh Bourne* (Bemersley: J. Bourne, 1834), 1:9-11, 2:2-8; Kendall, *Origin and History*, 1:177-201.

6. Preachers are described as "a most extraordinary variety," Bourne, *Memorable Camp Meeting*, 4; Bourne, *History*, 14; Bourne, *A Collection of Hymns for Camp Meetings, Revivals etc for use of Primitive Methodists* (Bemersley: J. Bourne, 1821).

The prayer meetings, class meetings, and the love feast—sometimes held later in the day after a camp meeting, were all highly participatory. It has been demonstrated that the proportion of Primitive Methodist members who were also local preachers was also very much higher in Primitive Methodism than it was in Wesleyan Methodism. Laypeople would baptize babies and preside at the sacrament of the Lord's Supper. This lay-led movement worked within a framework of response to mission opportunity, and not within a framework of "orders" or prohibition. The vicar of Sparholt, Berks, informed the bishop of Oxford that the local Ranters had told him that they would willingly come to church, if he would allow them to speak in church. The ethos of Primitive Methodism was such that this could happen in abundance.[7]

(3) Primitive Methodism developed from a domestic setting. While cottage prayer meetings were taking place in the Harriseahead area, praying and preaching was also being established in a kitchen at Tunstall, one of the pottery towns. The strength of the lower orders lay in their numbers. When the workers prayed, not only was the employer an outsider looking in, but so was the traveling preacher. They all prayed simultaneously, they all prayed out loud, and they each prayed in their own words. From Harriseahead the sound of prayer was heard at times a mile and a half away at Mow Cop. Hugh Bourne commented dryly, "Anyone who could make out his own voice in that lot must have had a pretty good ear." This common expression of emotion strengthened the bonds that the worshipers shared in this extremely clannish experience. However, at the same time these cottagers were also remarkably open to others who shared a common background and common problems. Those who in the upheaval of society had lost their land through enclosure, their jobs through industrialization, and their families through migration found a warm welcome, and new family ties were quickly established in the cottage meeting. Of course, in tied cottages[8] the tenant could face eviction for such activity, and the holding of such meetings was both a risk and an act of defiance. At Tunstall, where disillusioned Wesleyan Mr. Smith, who must have been one of the

7. Stephen G. Hatcher, "The Sacrament of the Lord's Supper in Early Primitive Methodism," *Proceedings of the Wesley Historical Society* 47 (1990): 221-31; Henry Pelling, *Popular Politics and Society in Late Victorian Britain* (London: Macmillan, 1968), 21.
8. "Tied cottages" were "tied to the job"—that is, housing that comes with the job.

wealthiest people in the Tunstall community, backed the embry-
onic Primitive group, the situation was far more secure; however,
such meetings were still interpreted as an act of defiance, with the
risk that the participants might forfeit their membership in the
Methodist Church.[9]

(4) Primitive Methodism offered secular education to the disadvantaged. When Jabez Bunting visited Sheffield in 1808, he was
shocked to see the children learning writing as well as reading in
the Sunday school. The argument of the "respectable" denominations was that it was proper to teach reading on a Sunday because
one was thereby teaching that child to read the Bible. What was not
"proper" was to teach writing and arithmetic. These subjects were
secular. It would be a shameful thing for a child to learn something
on a Sunday that might be used by that child to improve his station
in life! James Steele had created a similar sense of outrage in the
Tunstall Wesleyan Sunday school by teaching reading, writing, and
arithmetic to working-class children who were too busy to come
during the week after six days of labor totaling seventy-two hours,
and too tired to come in the evening. Bourne was determined that
working-class children would have a rudimentary education, and
promoted Sunday schools within his denomination for all he was
worth. Working-class people knew that Sunday school really was
the place to be if opportunity was to be seized in life. Even when
the state took over primary school education fully in 1870, the
strong bond between working people and Sunday school was such
that they would "send" their children for another three or four
generations.[10]

(5) The need for rest. At first sight, the prosecution of Sabbath
breakers through magistrates' courts might be seen as a reactionary
course. John Wesley and David Simpson both tried to turn back the
tide of the commercialization of Sunday, and William Clowes followed in this tradition. He was part of a movement that tried to
stamp out Sunday trading—including the Sunday opening of public houses. However, the circuit steward in the Burslem Wesleyan

9. *Deed Poll of the Primitive Methodist Connexion, 4 February 1830* (Bemersley: J. Bourne,
1837), 8-9; Kendall, *The Origin and History*, 1:106-10.

10. Thomas P. Bunting, *Life of Jabez Bunting, DD* (London: Woolmer, 1887), 295, 307; W. R.
Ward, ed., *The Early Correspondence of Jabez Bunting 1820-29* (London: Royal Historical
Society, 1972), 76-77; Handbill, Annual Sunday School Sermon, Tunstall 1811; William
Walker, *Wesley Place Sunday School, Tunstall, Centenary Souvenir 1799-1899* (Tunstall: E. H.
Eardley, 1900), 8; *Minutes* (British) 1808, Q25.

Circuit was a wine and spirit merchant who supplied the Sunday traders, and he clearly felt threatened by these bigots (as he regarded them). The Wesleyan superintendent reflected on the source of his quarterly paycheck, the honor of the circuit steward, and everything else that was in danger of being undermined. Clowes was threatened with expulsion unless he desisted. However, the action that Clowes was taking had been far from narrow. Sunday was believed to be precious for God. It was even more precious for working people, because it was about the only thing that they had. The loss of Sunday as a day of rest, after the cruel exploitation of the other six, was just unthinkable.[11]

(6) Female preachers. Women were far less well educated than men, and men were determined to keep it that way. Yet Wesley had given cautious encouragement to female preaching. Wesleyan Methodism clamped down on these female preachers shortly after Wesley's death, leaving a reservoir of frustrated female preacher talent—they had been called and were just waiting to be used. Undoubtedly part of their role was that of "mother in Israel." The small man driven to the edge of poverty and economic distress found comfort in the presence of such figures. That, however, is only part of the picture; even those females who were formidable figures found the going as itinerants extremely hard, and the combination of annual child bearing with the itinerant life often led to an even earlier grave. Primitive Methodists believed in this role for scriptural reasons, and Hugh Bourne wrote a tract in support of the practice of preaching and itineracy that in part followed the thinking of Margaret Fell, the early Quaker. Like so many things that the Primitive Methodists stood for, that which was thoroughly biblical was also thoroughly for the benefit of a disadvantaged group. Oppressed women were ennobled, poor lives were enriched.[12]

(7) A belief that God's interest was universal. The prophets of the eighth century (B.C.E.), such as Amos and Hosea, recognized that

---

11. Ernest M. Howse, *Saints in Politics* (London: Allen & Unwin, 1971), 119-24; William Clowes, *Journals* (London: Hallam & Holliday, 1844), 47-52: John T. Wilkinson, *William Clowes 1780-1851* (London: Epworth, 1951), 21.

12. Paul W. Chilcote, *John Wesley and the Women Preachers of Early Methodism* (Metuchen, N.J.: Scarecrow Press, 1991); Deborah M. Valenze, *Prophetic Sons and Daughters* (Princeton: Princeton University Press, 1985), 101; Hugh Bourne, "Remarks on the Ministry of Women," in John Walford, *Memoirs of the Life and Labours of the Late Venerable Hugh Bourne* (London: King, 1855-56), 1:172-77; Margaret Fell, *Women's Speaking Justified* (London: s.n., 1667).

God's interest was universal and by no means limited to Israel. Primitive Methodism had a wider view of where God was at work than Wesleyan Methodism. This is seen supremely in their concern for the poor. In all sorts of ways, the Primitive Methodists lived in a bigger world. The Wesleyans rejected Lorenzo Dow—partly because his visit to England was unofficial and he was unauthorized, partly because he was American, and partly because he was thoroughly Republican in his sympathies. They refer to him in their minutes as "a visiting American." Forty years later, when James Caughey visited England and breathed considerable life into an ailing Wesleyan Methodism, he was nonetheless similarly rejected. The Wesleyan Conference reiterated the earlier minutes that it had passed in relation to Dow. It was as if Wesleyan Methodism and visiting Americans were doomed not to mix. The small group who met with Dow and instigated that first English camp meeting does not seem to have had these hang-ups about Dow. Perhaps if the Republican revolution that he was judged to represent had come, these simple Primitive Methodists would have had far less to fear![13]

(8) An identification with the righteousness of God. There are a lot of parallels between the eighth-century prophets and the Primitive Methodists. Captain Edward Anderson, a sea captain of wide experience, was one of the prime movers behind the first camp meeting. It was he who hoisted a flag to guide visitors to its location, and recited poetry when they got there. In Anderson's *The Vices of the Times* there is exposure for some of the usual targets of popular Protestant piety—elaborate dress, fortune-telling, drunkenness, and lax sexual morality. His sternest words, however, were on behalf of those who had suffered loss of property rights through enclosure, and whose grievances cried to heaven like the laborers of the St. James Epistle (James 5:1-6). Not only did Anderson see economic doom and divine judgment pending for those who had built large farms at their neighbors' expense, but he pointed to the detail of their justly ignominious end:

> If all the greatest rogues within this land
> Suffered for all the wicked schemes they planned

---

13. Hull Wesleyan Methodist Circuit Minutes QM (28 December 1846); John Kent, *Holding the Fort* (London: Epworth, 1978), 79, 127; *Minutes* (British) 1847, Q39 (Visiting stranger from America); *Protest in favour of the Rev. James Caughey* (Sheffield: s.n., 1846).

Some that in coaches ride, would ride in carts,
And on a gallows tree have their deserts;
Abroad for enemies we need not roam,
We find our greatest enemies at home.[14]

(9) The proclamation of a present salvation. Experience was at the heart of Methodism, from Wesley's heart strangely warmed onwards. Primitive Methodism rediscovered this experience because it lived and preached in a world where its hearers knew daily what it meant to be lost or saved. Wherever life was likely to be beset with sudden danger or death, in addition to the short nasty brutish lives that all working people experienced, the gospel as preached by the Primitive Methodists was greeted most responsively. The coal and lead miners gambled daily with death, as did the east coast fishermen. Each day they did not know in the morning whether they would live to see the night. Each day they were either saved or lost. So the preacher spoke spiritually about themes that belonged to their real world, and the identification was complete.

They understood that the whole goal of life was to enjoy a present salvation, because yesterday's salvation would not do. The purpose of worship was to "get into faith" in order that this present experience could be encountered once more. In a context reminiscent of the Tractarians, but expressed at an earlier period, one is conscious of a specific route to grace with struggle, insistence, and victory, within a thoroughly dynamic context. Later in the nineteenth century, the Anglo-Catholics who also embraced Christian Socialism represent another area of affinity.[15]

(10) The proclamation of a full salvation. Wesley proclaimed a full salvation, and came to believe both in its quest and experience. In the early years of the nineteenth century some Wesleyan Methodists were not so sure. At the same time, Primitive Methodism believed itself to be a true successor to Wesley, and was

---

14. Edward Anderson, *Vices of the Times, A Poem* (Hull: J. Hutchinson, 1825), 7, 23-30. See also *Hull Packet* (25 January 1831), "Agricultural distress."

15. E. J. Hobsbawm, *Primitive Rebels* (Manchester University Press, 1971), 136: "the religion of the poor and insecure seems to require a sharp contrast between the gold of the redeemed and the flame-shot black of the damned." For a discussion of how the phrase "A full, free, and present salvation" relates to Wesley's teaching, see: *Proceedings of the Wesley Historical Society* 41.5 (1978): 166, 42.2 (1979): 64, 43.6 (1982): 182f; *Primitive Methodist Magazine* (1829): 369, (1830): 131-36, (1831): 145.

conscious that despite Wesleyan hesitation, many were still actively seeking the experience of sanctification. So it is not surprising that there is considerable evidence that some Wesleyan Methodists found this experience of sanctification within the context of Primitive Methodism, simply because they believed in it, but it was not on offer back home. There is also evidence that within the progress of a revival, a sanctification phase would follow a justification phase, thereby keeping the revival alive and the believer edified. However, this seeking for the moral high ground also has a considerable amount to do with being poor and oppressed. Of course, the respectable poor had their pride, but with a full, free, and present salvation they were in the Kingdom while others were outside. The love-feast itself was the opportunity for this experience of perfect love to be expressed in community. It was not possible to be present without marveling at the privilege of the "poor, the crippled, the blind and the lame," and those who had come in from the "country roads and lanes"; while others who had clearly declined the invitation were outside (Luke 14:15-24).[16]

(11) Identification with radical politics. In 1831 James Acland, who had moved to Hull that year, provided a spark that would ignite the smoldering political grievances. Soon the local newspapers would be speaking of the visible results of "a riotous and tumultuous assemblage of ill-disposed persons." Acland would challenge the corporation and the hypocrisy of Wesleyan Methodists. Among the latter, Alderman Avison Terry featured regularly in Acland's paper *The Portfolio:*

> A performance will take place at the Methodist Chapel, on Sunday next, under the direction of Mr. Alderman Turkey-cock . . . He will personify Judas Iscariot—if he can borrow a money bag. . . . By the wave of his magisterial wand, he will convert a charity-school into a stable, and a respectable old man into a pauper.[17]

No wonder that when the magistrates called out 800 special constables against Acland's followers in 1832, Acland's paper would

---

16. Clowes, *Journals*, 59, 287; *Primitive Methodist Magazine* (1828): 162; Walford, *Memoirs*, 1:101-2; Stephen G. Hatcher, "The Origin and Expansion of Primitive Methodism in the Hull Circuit 1819–1851" (University of Manchester Ph.D. thesis, 1993), 251-68.

17. Hull Portfolio 13 March 1832, 103.

also report that members of religious communities wei
those actively opposing him, with the strongest opposition
from Wesleyan local preachers and leaders.

There is not a hint of criticism of the Primitive Methodist.
Acland, though he does not allude to them as a group positively
either. This may lead one to assume that they were politically neu-
tral. This was not the case! Acland published in his paper a list of
those who were supporting him as candidate for Church Warden at
Holy Trinity Church at Easter 1832. A number of the names of those
who are indicated as voting for the man who had brought this
"quiet old town to its near parlous state" can be clearly identified
as leading members of the Primitive Methodist Chapel on Mill
Street:

Thomas Whiting, Labourer, High Street.
William Westoby, Bricklayer, Mill Street.
William Roberts, Labourer, West Street.
William Wilkinson, Labourer, High Street.
Thomas Longman, Smith, Edgar Street.
William Glenton, Shoemaker, West Street.
William Suddards, Pawnbroker, Trippet.
Edward Anderson, Gentleman (former Sea Captain), North
    Street.
Richard Walker, Clerk, Postern Gate.[18]

The reactionary establishment line of Hull Wesleyan Methodists
was news; the radical progressive involvement of the Primitive
Methodists passed without comment. Such a position was natural
for Methodists after all.

(12) The Trades Union Movement. Preachers who were arrested
for preaching on the streets would sometimes continue preaching
through the prison bars. At Huddersfield, for instance, William
Taylor and Sister Parry did just this from a lockup adjacent to the
market square, and the responsive simple hearers of the Word
pushed food back through the bars in return. Thus the preachers
experienced the savagery of a system under which their congregations groaned daily. Those who were local preachers and rooted
in just one locality, like Joseph Capper the Tunstall blacksmith and

---

18. Hull Portfolio 28 April 1832, 172-77; 26 May 1832, 220-24; June 1832, 234.

Chartist activist, were particularly able to engage with the system consistently, proactively, and progressively. Capper perceived that the restricted franchise and low wages went hand in hand. To most of his contemporaries he was a Christian, a man of peace, and a hero. However, he finished up in Stafford Gaol for two years following the Pottery Riots of 1842, vested interests having found him guilty of sedition.[19]

As these conflicts continued, many others from the ranks discovered a dignity as children of God, a dignity then denied them by the system, and were given the confidence to challenge authority. When the Durham miners went on strike in 1844, the coal owners decided to take a tough line and evicted the strikers from their tied cottages. The membership of the Durham Primitive Methodist Circuit was cut by more than half as a consequence. The struggle of the miners for better conditions was the struggle of the chapel leaders and members equally. John Wilson would rise through the ranks from Sunday school teacher and local preacher to Durham miners' leader, county councilor, and as one of the first miners' leaders to sit in Parliament. For Wilson it had all begun because two elderly Primitive Methodist miners called at his door on their way to the pit. They did not reproach him for his hangover, but saw the potential within him, and engaged him in work at the chapel. From that day on he was a changed man, and for the rest of his life a personal religious conversion and his quest to transform the conditions encountered on the Durham coalfield went hand in hand. No religious group played a more significant part in providing trade union leaders among the coal miners and the agricultural workers than did the Primitive Methodists. Among the agricultural laborers, the work of Joseph Arch and George Edwards was particularly significant.[20]

---

19. An Old Potter (Charles Shaw), *When I was a Child* (London: Methuen and Co., 1903), 141-81.

20. R. F. Wearmouth, *Methodism and the Working Class Movements of England 1800–1850* (London: Epworth, 1937), 187-88. Eviction reduced the membership of Durham circuit from 1,500 in 1843 to 520 in 1844; cf. John Wilson, *Memories of a Labour Leader*, with a new introduction by John Burnett (Firle, Sussex: Caliban Books, 1980 [1910 ori.]); John Wilson, *A History of the Durham Miners' Association 1870–1904* (Durham: Veitch and Sons, 1907), 365; Joseph Arch, *Autobiography*, ed. J. G. O'Leary (London: Macgibben & Kee, 1966); Joseph Arch, *The Story of his Life* (London: Hutchinson, 1898); and George Edwards, *From Crow Scaring to Westminster* (London: Labour Publishing Company, 1922).

The Return of Radical Methodism

The skill of the early Primitive Methodists was not just to do what Wesley had done, but to take his spirit also and apply it to their own rapidly changing world. They did so just one generation after his death, while the world today stands seven generations from 1807 and eight generations from 1791. Through the work of the Methodist Chapel and Museum of Primitive Methodism at Englesea Brook, an attempt is now being made to respond to the challenge of doing again what these early Primitive Methodists did.[21]

Part of the purpose of the museum is to gather artifacts that express the spirit of this early movement. For instance, one of the prize exhibits at Englesea Brook is the very pulpit used by William Clowes and others in Mr. Smith's kitchen, Tunstall, from 1808. Crudely adapted from a chest of drawers, it serves as a reminder of the movement's homely, humble origins.

Thomas Russell looks out from behind bars and at the push of a button will explain why he was imprisoned for three months with hard labor. By his side is a list of other Primitive Methodists who were persecuted for their faith, and a long list of names supplied by Amnesty International of prisoners of conscience today.

Englesea Brook has lived on the frontier of opposition and financial uncertainty, but most important of all it has lived on that frontier where the church should meet the world and faith should meet unbelief. For the last few years approximately one hundred visits to local schools have been made each year for assembly or classroom time. Twelve hundred pupils also visited Englesea Brook last season for a day visit. It is always rewarding to spend time with young people, and particularly so when through costume and role play they perceive the important part that faith can play in young lives.

Englesea Brook has just purchased an adjacent cottage to house a rapidly growing library and to provide overnight accommodation for those who wish to study, look at Methodist heritage, or just enjoy the peace of the rural setting. It sells thousands of secondhand books in the course of the year, and is always keen to hold Bible study sessions and study days.

---

21. For more on this work see www.engleseabrook-museum.org.uk

Englesea Brook as a village was once the home of the rural poor, but changing patterns of living and changing property prices mean that this is no longer so. It is very important therefore that the feet of the project are kept firmly on the ground in order to continue to give expression to that spirit of Primitive Methodism. This will be true as long as the workers for the project spend as much time with people in Stoke-on-Trent and Crewe as part of the outreach program as at Englesea Brook. The full-time development officer lives in inner city working-class Tunstall, his children attend the local working-class school, where 40 percent of the children have free school dinners, and he daily rides the buses to go to his appointments.

The Englesea Brook project, as an expression of the venturesome innovative spirit of Primitive Methodism, is judged to be a success. That success would be complete if those who applaud also recognize why—it simply seeks to be true to the radical origin of the Methodist movement as a whole.

For the Future

It has been suggested that the Spirit was upon a pragmatic Wesley who desired only that God should engage creatively with human need. The Primitive Methodists received the baton and similarly grounded their activity in the realities of human life. Bourne as much as Wesley had a "messianic call." But what of the compulsion of such a call for the future? I believe that the visible signs of its expression include the following:

(1) There will be more experimental projects and fewer traditional churches. The straitjacket will be left behind. Many of these projects will not survive, but some will, and they will reveal new patterns for the twenty-first century.

(2) There will be no major new building schemes, but the adaptation of existing buildings in a way that is more in harmony with the principles of conservation. Domestic buildings and nonreligious secular building will be increasingly used. A church that thinks it has half a million pounds or more for a new building will think again, and put resources instead into evangelists, prophets, and workers with young people. Besides, in an ecumenical context new buildings are all just likely to be wasted.

(3) So many churches have lost so many young people that a whole generation now lives in total ignorance of the gospel message. This critical situation will occasion a response that is in the spirit of the early Methodist "days of fasting and nights of prayer." No one knew better than Hugh Bourne that the highest priority was to engage with young people. There is still an open door to many schools. While there is time, enter in. The motivation is in the worth of the young lives that are in danger of being wasted. It is certainly not to save the church!

(4) The great threat to human life, and indeed to all life on our planet in the future, is an environmental one. Time is running out within a society looking for prophetic leadership. Global warming, the depletion of natural resources, and the continuing growth of population are currently raising the disaster stakes. Only lives lived with integrity, voices raised prophetically, and groups acting concertedly have any relevance at all.

Jesus, John Wesley, Hugh Bourne, and the early Primitive Methodists, including the Durham miners, all had a strong messianic call. Modern Methodists are part of this noble company when similarly they yearn to save souls, bodies, and their planet, honestly and relevantly, within a contemporary context.

One cannot "make" the Christian lifestyle. It is created by the Spirit when we personally and in community bind our life with the life of Christ and understand our life-history as a small part of God's great history of liberating the world.

CHAPTER 9

SOUTH AFRICAN VOICES RESHAPING METHODISM

CEDRIC MAYSON

Radical Methodists in South Africa, operating mainly outside of church structures, recognized the conflict between the inspiration and institutions of Christianity, and the dangers of the "pharisaic syndrome". The South African experience prompted a reassessment of the good news of Jesus about the kingdom of God. This good news embraces the collapse of oppressive empires and the growth of local societies. Contemporary Methodism will not be revitalized by taking the message of the margins to the center, but by following the center of God's activity into the margins.

South Africa achieved political transformation in the 1994 democratic elections and has been seeking social transformation ever since. Radical Methodists have been very involved,[1] but with a few exceptions[2] *radical Methodists have been ministers who have withdrawn from the active ministry through resignation, transfers to other jobs, or early retirement.* Unknown numbers of laity also despaired of doing

---

1. Through various government structures, the Truth and Reconciliation Commission, the Anti-Corruption Forum, the African National Congress Commission of Religious Affairs, the National Religious Leaders Forum, the new national Moral Regeneration Movement, and many other initiatives at a local level.

2. Such as the Presiding Bishop the Reverend H. Mvume Dandala and one or two of his colleagues.

constructive work inside the church. Thus the church became a site of struggle between the radicals who saw God at work in the transformation of the attitudes and structures of society, and the conservatives who wanted to run a church. Ecclesiastical institutions agreed that society needed transforming but their emphasis was on promoting their own structures, traditions, rituals, attitudes, and obsession with individual salvation. Centuries of indoctrination in "churchiness" condemned many church people to follow versions of Christianity unrecognizable to its founder.

This painful split was clearly recognized in 1985, at the height of the struggle to liberate ourselves from oppression, when a group of radical Christian South Africans—including many Methodists—issued a booklet called *Challenge to the Church*, which was soon known as *The Kairos Document*. Early in the document it was stressed that "what the present crisis shows us is that *the church is divided.* . . . There are Christians on both sides of the conflict—and some who are trying to sit on the fence."[3]

Such separate development may seem natural to Europeans or North Americans reared in colonial attitudes, but is anathema to those with a holistic African understanding of life.

Inspiration Versus Institution

Christianity has always experienced tensions between inspiration and institution. Some, inspired by Jesus of Nazareth, sought to follow his Way. Others focused on running religious bodies which became "trapped within the iron cage of history" in protecting their power, possessions, and privileges. This clash between radicals and conservatives underscored the split between Anglicanism and John Wesley in the Great Awakening of eighteenth-century Britain.

Most of us are conditioned to equate "proclaiming the Gospel" with "promoting the Church" and many feel cheated if it is suggested that God is working in the world outside the church, as if the God they own has been hijacked. Jesus knew that everyone was spiritual but not everyone was religious, and proclaimed his gospel in the world among the people, not in church.

3.*The Kairos Document, Challenge to the Church: a Theological Comment on the Political Crisis in South Africa*, 2nd edition (Braamfontein: Skotaville Publishers; & Grand Rapids: Eerdmans, 1986), 1.

The Pharisaic Syndrome

Huge crowds found that Jesus made more sense than the official religious leaders, whom he criticized for their worship of Mammon (Mark 4:18-19; 10:25; Luke 16:13-15; 18:24; Matt. 6:26), traditional institutions (Mark 7:5-9), and fundamentalism (Matt. 5:21-48; Mark 2:21). The Pharisees were a pious and godly sect whose desire for lives of purity fostered an absolutist anti-god religion. Jesus called them a brood of vipers, a wicked generation, blind guides (Matt. 3:7; 5:20; 23:13-36). These interwoven facets are a pharisaic syndrome that continues today.

Many still worship money as the focus of life, truss up the Spirit of God in religious traditions, and promote false spiritual fundamentals. The Pharisees' insistence that their way is the one and only way to God is cruel, uncaring, heretical bunk. Pharisees move the focus from doing the truth and enacting a liberated society, to worshiping the idols of money, "churchianity," and false fundamentalist emotions. They worship a dead God incarcerated in out-of-date doctrines, a museum piece periodically dusted off and re-embalmed like Lenin's corpse, not a permanently alive and resurrected experience. Pharisees are motivated not by faith but by heresy, not by hope but by despair, not by love but by fear and violence. Fundamentalism is the HIV of the soul, sweeping through the whole community, opening us to the opportunistic infections of western apostasy. It is a hocus-pocus religion, a false superstition designed to support oppressors. Wesley said:

> I find more profit in sermons on either good manners or good works than in what are vulgarly called Gospel sermons. That term has now become a mere cant word: I wish none of our society would use it. Let but a pert, self-sufficient animal, that has neither sense nor grace, bawl out something about Christ, or his blood, or justification by faith, and his hearers cry out: "What a fine gospel sermon!"[4]

Jesus had to confront and reject the temptation to become a Pharisee himself.

---

4. Letter to Mary Bishop (18 October 1778), *Letters* (Telford) 6:326-27.

The South African Experience

Methodism came to South Africa through soldiers in the British Occupation of the Cape in 1806. The British Conference appointed ministers in 1816. Massive missionary expansion in the black community happened as Africans responded to the inspiration of Jesus, who makes a great deal of sense within basic human African spirituality (which we are rediscovering today). But Africans were reluctant to embrace the imported colonial ecclesiastical institutions, and within two generations thousands broke away to form independent African Indigenous churches, many led by Methodists. Then came apartheid.

Three problems emerged in South African Methodism: oppression, politics, and authoritarianism.

(1) *Oppression had to be recognized and named as evil.* Many church people accepted contemporary oppressive views on race, women, and economic exploitation. They embraced a type of "state theology," which was, in reality, "simply the theological justification of the status quo with its racism, capitalism, and totalitarianism."[5]

Epic struggles to ordain black Africans and appoint them as superintendents, presidents, and bishops lasted over a century. Benevolent, kind, white liberals thought that blacks could become like them after a few centuries of white tutelage and resisted giving blacks the same teaching, stipends, and prestigious pulpits. Many still do. A 1958 white proposal to divide the church on racial grounds was only narrowly defeated.[6] Many sincerely believed that apartheid would protect and promote Christian civilization, a view strongly supported in the United States and the United Kingdom.[7] The role of women was to manage homes and raise money for churches; and of course, everyone should give charity to help the poor blacks to survive. Radicals said these were oppressive attitudes of a widespread evil system that had to be named and overthrown in the name of God. Comfortable respectable Christians were outraged.

(2) *Political involvement was crucial.* There was strong opposition within the church when the Christian Institute and the South African

---

5. *Kairos Document*, 3.

6. Thus saving Methodism from the anguish of the churches that did divide on racial grounds and are now enduring the traumas of joining up again.

7. Of course, no one today will admit to having supported apartheid.

Council of Churches produced "The Message to the People of South Africa," which rejected apartheid, beginning a thirty-year struggle.[8] Many believed that the church should not get involved in politics (except by supporting the status quo), but radicals maintained that "changing the structure of a society is fundamentally a matter of politics. It requires a political strategy based upon a clear political or social analysis. . . . It is into this political situation that the church has to bring the gospel."[9]

The problem was not a matter of personal guilt but of structural injustice. The message of Jesus was not confined to private individuals but promised a collective transformation. We believed that the liberation struggle was a righteous and godly act in itself, and our task was to get involved in the actual struggle, not to start a cleaned-up and more churchified version:

> It is into this political situation that the church has to bring the gospel. Not as an alternative solution to our problems as if the gospel provided us with a non-political solution to political problems . . . but quite simply [to] participate in the struggle for liberation and a just society. . . . The church must avoid becoming a "Third Force," a force between the oppressor and the oppressed.[10]

During this period, right-wing pentecostal fundamentalism began to dominate Methodism as a cop-out from confronting the reality of political oppression. Many radicals were sickened by the substitution of emotionalism for theological insight, and by the commitment to a conformist church rather than a transformed society.

In the struggle we discovered a common purpose with other Christians, Muslims, Jews, Hindus, agnostics, and African traditional believers. Because God was in the liberation struggle with all its problems and passions, we all joined that godly struggle and then did our theology inside it. Jesus knew very well that it was only by doing the works of God that we could know the doctrine (John 7:17). Wesley would have agreed: "Some great truths, as the being and attributes of God, and the difference between moral good

---

8. See *A Message to the People of South Africa* (Braamfontein: South African Council of Churches).

9. *Kairos Document*, 15.

10. Ibid., 15, 28, 29.

and evil, were known in some measure to the heathen world. The traces of them are to be found in all nations."[11]

(3) *The authority of the church leadership had to be challenged.* Many loyal church members were reluctant to recognize that there was a ruling clique in the church which had to be challenged.[12] The process of challenging that clique began with such movements as "The Time is Now,"[13] and included Black Consciousness, Black Theology, Feminist Theology, Contextual Theology, and African Theology. Ruling churchmen sincerely believed they were the leaders of Christianity in Africa, and the pharisaic syndrome precluded any thought that God could speak through anyone else.

For most, this blindness to the faith dynamic was because they never personally joined in the peoples' struggle. Many deliberately withdrew from it ("I cannot endanger my family, congregation, pension, etc.") and others seldom went further than wordy discussions. They were a protected species with little experience of poverty, jail, violence, or confrontation. The *Kairos Document* said that the cause of this blindness "must be sought in the *type of faith and spirituality* that has dominated church life for centuries. As we all know, spirituality has tended to be an other-worldly affair. . . . This kind of spirituality, when faced with the present crisis, leaves so many Christians and church leaders in a state of near paralysis."[14]

We live in a partisan age when the sense of being part of the whole human community is undermined by authoritarian insistence that our race, religion, sex, class, culture, motor car, running shoes, or theology sets us apart from others, making our differences more important than our similarities. Despite his immense personal authority, Jesus never imposed religion or creed on anyone. His invitation was to find God's Ruling Power everywhere in anyone. Likewise, while John Wesley had firm opinions on many subjects, he would have nothing to do with such intolerance:

> The Methodists alone do not insist on your holding this or that opinion, but they think and let think. Neither do they impose any particular mode of worship, but you may continue to worship in your former manner, be that what it may.[15]

---

11. Sermon 85, "On Working Out Our Own Salvation," §1, *Works* 3:199.
12. After all, they also provided our bread and butter.
13. An attempt to stir renewal in the 1960s.
14. *Kairos Document*, 16.
15. *Journal* (18 May 1788), *Works* 24:85.

We are not called to make "Methodists" or produce "a Christian answer," but to expound God operating in the whole of human community, enabling people to recognize the Spirit in their own religious, social, cultural, economic, or political communities. Dr. Frances Young of the British Methodist Church states the matter clearly:

> It is not by accepting traditional formulations as God given and unquestionable that we join the band of witnesses in the New Testament and the early church, but by wrestling with the problem of expressing intelligently in our own contemporary environment, our personal testimony to the redemptive effect of faith in Jesus of Nazareth.[16]

Those who substitute obedience to religious authorities for belief in a God acting in this world soon lose confidence that change can actually happen. It threatens their authority, too. It is the poor and outcast who know change will happen, like the students in Soweto, the poor, and the women. Throughout South Africa, people recognized the evil of apartheid, the necessity of political action, and the need to confront the leadership of the church, and began to gather together in small groups. They had a dozen different names and orientations, but together were the seedbeds of the revolution.

Rediscovering the Basileia

Christians in the liberation struggle found they had to reassess the evidence of Jesus' actual teaching, the inspiration that came before the institution, the faith expressed in liberation theology that arose within the struggle. Many were shocked to find so much of Christianity was invented by the church centuries after "Jesus came to Galilee proclaiming the good news of God, and saying, 'The time is fulfilled, and the kingdom of God has come near; repent, and believe in the good news'" (Mark 1:14).

Many today have still not heard that good news. They know about an ecclesiastical kingdom in terms of church; a spiritual king-

---

16. Frances Young, "A Cloud of Witnesses," in *The Myth of God Incarnate*, edited by John Hick (London: SCM, 1977), 30.

dom in terms of soul; a heavenly kingdom of life after death; and a future kingdom at the end of the age; but not the good news of Jesus about the dynamic ruling power of God operating among people on earth here and now. The phrase "kingdom of God" is a bad translation of the Greek word *basileia*, for Jesus was not announcing an autocratic male monarchy. The word means *ruling power*, not a state or place. Jesus proclaimed the tremendous good news that the ruling power of God (RPG) was operating in human society, and lived his life on that basis.

The RPG is a movement emerging in society, not a rule imposed on it. It is not a program but a vision; a driving, inspiriting experience of belief; a pressure operating in the community that produces programs: dynamic not static. The RPG operates in powerless situations among poor and marginalized people: the rich cannot make head nor tail of it without insights from the poor. The RPG cannot be imposed from the top but arises from the bottom. It empowers. It challenges. It is a struggle. It moves by *kairos* times—that is, when the moment is ready.

Followers of Jesus have to proclaim the RPG operating in Africa today, the vision that determines its priorities and the faith that releases its power. The *basileia* is still good news to the poor and oppressed, and a mystery to many of the rich and powerful. Those of us involved in the liberation struggle gained a unique insight into the meaning of the gospel and its understanding of the world. Facing oppression releases the RPG into your understanding and activities, naming and confronting the devil, discovering a new vision, a new faith, a new commitment, a new power. It carries with it an assurance of the inevitable collapse of the old political, economic, and theological empires that stand in the way. In the darkest night it sees the promise of dawn.[17]

The Collapse of Empires

The confrontation between oppressors and the RPG has surfaced in every age. Almost at random, we can note Friedrich Heer's comment on the medieval world.

---

17. Like the confidence that buoyed people up in prison or at funerals.

Contemporary medieval society, whose daily life was warfare, unrest, tumult, hatred, envy, and the lust for power, all those sinister beasts of prey whom Dante saw stalking through the world, was confronted with its greatest challenge . . . in Francis of Assisi who taught the good news for what it was: a message of joy and love, God dwelling at peace with men.[18]

People today are indoctrinated to believe that Earth is ruled by might and wealth, that globalized capitalism, political control, and religious domination are permanent features which the godly must support.[19] We have been taught history from the viewpoint of rich and powerful conquerors storming across the pages to write their names in political, economic, or ecclesiastical ink, endorsing a social Darwinism of the survival of the fittest. It is nonsense. The RPG has broken through constantly to deflate oppressive empires like punctured balloons and prompt the growth of ordinary people. History needs re-writing from the experience of the poor, weak, and oppressed who have determined the contours of history.[20] The princes of political, military, economic, and ecclesiastical might have been pulled from their thrones, the proud of heart routed, the rich sent empty away, and the hungry filled with good things, including education, health, housing, holidays, security, and liberation (Luke 1:50-53). Thus, the *Kairos Document* exhorted:

The church should not only pray for a change of government, it should also mobilise its members in every parish to begin to think and work and plan for a change of government in South Africa. We must begin to look ahead and begin working now with firm hope and faith for a better future.[21]

The current anti-human focus is the empire of transnational corporations, the dictatorship controlling the globe's capital. It is not designed to improve the quality of life for people. Ninety-five percent of transactions which wash trillions of dollars round the globe's financial system every day are not about food and housing and health and education, but simply financial speculation, motivated

---

18. Friedrich Heer, *The Medieval World* (London: Weidenfeld and Nicolson, 1969), 181.
19. "We did not design the market economy," expostulated an American Methodist to me. "It is just the way the world is."
20. Jesus saw them as custodians of the basiliea.
21. *Kairos Document*, 30.

by greed not grace. It is the self-centered worship of the idol of money. It needs to be named as such, shunned as such, and over-turned as such. Our response should be the same as it was to apartheid:

> The [apartheid] regime has lost any legitimacy it might have had in the eyes of the people. . . . [It] is unreformable. . . . A regime that is in principle the enemy of the people cannot suddenly begin to rule in the interests of all the people. It can only be replaced by another government . . . with an explicit mandate to govern in the interests of all the people.[22]

The RPG puts a directional bias like gravity into human society, and even while oppressors drive vast military destruction, global-ize increasing poverty, and call the faithful to peace while aggres-sively asserting their own religious empires, the world is being swept by unprecedented commitments to development, to emanci-pating women, to removing racism, to saving the environment, and to establishing a common ground of being. The empires are unable to neutralize the progressive movements[23] arising through-out the world, led by the poor and the unchurched. The political, economic, and religious structures need a revolution if they are to take an active part in it.[24] The RPG calls us to a global transfor-mation.

Center and Margins

Radicals on the margins of Methodism cannot revitalize its cen-tral structures. You cannot put new wine into old wineskins, because the world does not work that way. The margins are mov-ing away from the gravitational pull of the old world into that of a new world, and if the central structures want life and fulfillment, they must move into the margins where the weight of the RPG is deployed. A church moving forward must support the struggle

---

22. Ibid., 23, 24.

23. e.g., in Seattle, Geneva, Durban, Johannesburg—or in Methodism.

24. Future people will not ask who knocked over the World Trade Center any more than they ask who knocked over the Tower of Babel or the Coliseum. It is not the evil of the act that will register, but the sign of the times that has rejected an ungodly way of life promoted by Western politics, economics, and religion.

wherever it is happening, if it is to empower new political, economic, and theological forces. As the authors of the *Kairos Document* insisted:

> To be truly biblical our church leaders must adopt a theology that millions of Christians have already adopted—a biblical theology of direct confrontation with the forces of evil rather than a theology of reconciliation with sin and the devil.[25]

The gospel means obeying the ruling processes of God operating in the secular and collective human community where people are suffering from ignorance, poverty, disease, and oppression, not marketing exclusive religious institutions and individual salvation. Evil systems are normally eaten away from the roots, not overthrown (although this may happen). Oppressive empires fail because their inherent instability ensures an expiry date. They are rebuilt from the edges, not the top.

Most politicians and theologians work on the basis that because the collapse of the present world systems is unthinkable, they will not think about it, which means they also refuse to think of what must come in its place. By contrast, it is clear to the oppressed:

> The problem that we are dealing with here in South Africa is not simply a problem of personal guilt, it is a problem of structural injustice. People are suffering, people are being maimed and killed and tortured every day. . . . True justice, God's justice, demands a radical change of structures. This can only come from below, from the oppressed themselves.[26]

Ecclesiastical structures must research a total revamp of their practices and their theology. The people have spoken. Most find mainline religion uninspiring or downright false; many are outgrowing the temporary distraction of western pop Pentecostalism which is full of sound and fury but signifies nothing. Self-centered schemes of spiritual renewal may have marginal personal successes, but will remain middle-class distortions of the Way of Jesus until they envisage large-scale collective sanctification. As the *Kairos Document* recognized,

---

25. *Kairos Document*, 11.
26. Ibid., 12.

> Much of what we do in our church services has lost its relevance to the poor and the oppressed. Our services and sacraments have been appropriated to serve the need of the individual for comfort and security. Now these same church activities must be re-appropriated to serve the real religious needs of all the people and to further the liberating mission of God and the church in the world.[27]

Human renewal from Jesus and Mohammed to Marx and Castro has always been through small groups with a social purpose and a living experience. Jesus, the apostles, Paul, and Wesley accepted large congregations, but put their strength into empowering small groups of people in their homes and neighborhoods. We must look to similar small ecumenical and interfaith groups, with their feet placed firmly on the spirit level of human beings, committed to the collective sanctification of proclaiming the RPG, to banish poverty and empower a transformed society. Such groups are the source of hope. Tinyiko Maluleke, one of our modern prophets has written:

> A basic challenge for African Theology in this century is to find out how we might regain passion and compassion at what is happening all around; the courage and energy to act and act decisively, as well as the hope to see beyond the unacceptable present.[28]

This need is echoed in the *Kairos Document:*

> Most of the oppressed people in South Africa today and especially the youth do have hope. They are acting courageously and fearlessly because they have a sure hope that liberation will come. Often enough their bodies are broken but nothing can now break their spirit. But hope needs to be confirmed. Hope needs to be maintained and strengthened. Hope needs to be spread. The people need to hear it said again and again that God is with them.[29]

And So?

Can the experience of South African radical Christians have an impact on the wider world? Can Christians in the West grasp

---

27. Ibid., 29.
28. In Speckman et al., *Towards an Agenda*, 375.
29. *Kairos Cocument*, 26.

the truth that apartheid revealed what Western civilization is actually like? And that the *Kairos Document* does the same for Western Christianity?

Christendom is riddled with the pharisaic syndrome. The religious institutions of the West—Christian, Jewish, and Muslim—have been hijacked by political, economic, and theological oppressors and have rejected the great source of their common inspiration. The dictatorship of globalized capitalism (the greatest crime against humanity since slavery) is producing unprecedented suffering backed by oppressive but unstable political empires and confronted by millions of crucified people. Because God is like Jesus, resurrecting change is coming crashing in. The church is being challenged to get off its high horse, rediscover the good news of the RPG, and put its weight behind the poor and oppressed instead of seeking to justify or reform the oppressors.

From Africa we reach out to our church, and to the world, with hope. This will not save those organizations that have passed their sell-by date, but it promises a new lease of life to turn the world upside down. I am an African, not an American or European, and can only end this chapter from an African point of view. In 1997 a Methodist layman named Nelson Mandela said:

> The transformation of our country requires the closest possible cooperation between religious and political bodies, critically and wisely serving our people together. Neither political nor religious objectives can be achieved in isolation. They are held in a creative tension with common commitments. We are partners in the building of our nation.[30]

Three of the significant movements since then, represented in the acronyms NRLF, AU, and MRM, can each be seen in the context of the RPG. The National Religious Leaders Forum was formed in direct response to Mandela's call. It meets regularly to seek to work together, and twice a year meets with the President. The African Union is an initiative to unite and strengthen the whole continent to replace the ravages of colonialism and neo-colonialism with a new political and economic dispensation—and a recovery of spiritual power. The Moral Regeneration Movement is a new South

---

30. Nelson Mandela, Address to Religious Leaders, African National Congress, Johannesburg, 24 June, 1997.

African initiative that brings together government, all political parties, religions, business, labor, and all sectors of our society to seek moral regeneration as the basis of social transformation. Each of these movements was initiated by a political response to pressure from the grass roots. They will have profound economic effects, but are at heart a spiritual quest embracing all religions. The RPG was never more active.

The question that arises in South Africa is the same question that arises in the wider world—can the Methodist Church respond to the vision of the radicals in its midst? Or is Methodism too busy running the church to discover what it is running it for?

CHAPTER 10

RADICAL METHODISM

The Challenges of Partnership and Mutuality in the Task of Evangelizing Ghana

MERCY AMBA ODUYOYE

Methodism in Ghana began as a Bible study group made up of a few young men in Oguaa, a town situated on the west coast of Africa in the sector that was later named Gold Coast, now Ghana. Oguaa became Cape Coast and remains a stronghold of Methodism. In my lifetime, what these young men began has gone from being a Wesleyan Methodist mission to becoming the Methodist Church of Ghana, and lately taking on the episcopal order. But it has always been evangelical. The Bible study group called for Bibles and got missionaries in addition. The workers were both British and indigenous. Several Methodist societies have their roots in small study and prayer groups begun by Ghanaians. There have been several periods of intentional and intensive moves to evangelize the country. We are in another such phase. This is very appropriate because the roots of Methodism itself flow from a young people's Bible study group. I am referring, of course, to the Oxford antecedents of our church.

In exploring the challenges of partnership and mutuality, this chapter will focus not on origins either in England or Ghana, but on the present situation. The task of evangelizing Africa was seen as that of European missionary societies. There was no question of partnership or mutuality. There was no question as to whether the Africans wanted to be evangelized. All that mattered was Jesus' command: "Go ye . . ." (Matt. 28:19). Jesus is reported to have said "compel them to come in" (Luke 14:23), and no less a person than Augustine of Hippo used this parabolic saying to justify unilateral evangelization. The nineteenth- and twentieth-century missionaries to Africa did not exactly *compel*, but they did insist that when people "became Christian" they leave behind all things religious and cultural in their African background. The question of partnership did not arise; mission was a paternalistic endeavor. It was assumed to be necessary to save Africans from themselves and from their culture. Mutuality was inconceivable, for what could one learn from or gain as a benefit from such an abject person?

This exploration of the challenges of partnership and mutuality will be set against the general background of the evangelization of Africa, and of Ghana in particular. It will sweep widely, paying little attention to the specificity of denominational policies. Although I am a Methodist—in fact, I grew up in a manse—I see the challenges facing Christianity in Ghana in ecumenical rather than denominational terms. Indeed, making the oneness of the church visible is itself a prime challenge to partnership. The current multiplicity and variety of manifestations of the church and of Christianity can totally paralyze any thought of partnership, not to mention mutuality. So I will deal first with the relevance of the global ecumenical movement for the situation in Africa and Ghana. I see in ecumenism a move toward the mutuality and partnership in the task of evangelization that is so badly needed.

True Ecumenicity

Students of the history of Christianity may characterize the century just closed as the century of Christian ecumenism of councils and conferences, in which dialogue has become a central avenue for encounter of communities professing partnership and mutuality. The World Mission Conference of Edinburgh in 1910 focused on unity in the mission field, with a goal "That all may believe."

Ecumenism requires partnership and mutuality. Reflecting on the scene in Ghana as well as the relationship between partner churches from North and South, I get the sense that ecumenical relations operate bilaterally and across denominational lines. World confessional families, or better Christian world communions, come together in such groups as the World Alliance of Reformed Churches; and individual bodies like the Reformed Church in Switzerland form liaisons with the Presbyterian Church in Ghana, to their mutual benefit. What I look for in the next decades is that a body like the Reformed Church might undertake an evangelistic project to the benefit of *all* churches and even beyond into the wider community, "that the world may believe." My own community has some way to go in this regard. Methodists may come together in the World Methodist Council, but it does not take long in the practice of sharing resources for the continuing fault line between missions related to Methodism in the United States and those related to British Methodism to become clear, not to mention the splits within U.S. Methodism that reflect the history of racism in that setting.

Mutuality and partnership will grow out of—as well as become evidence of—the Eucharistic hospitality that we need to promote. This is the first item on my "wish list" for the church's life. The divisions at the Lord's Table here in Ghana are not our creation; we have been schooled into them. They reflect our relationship to Western churches, even if we no longer feel drawn to these historical divides. When we turn our attention to the relationships between the Western and Eastern churches, the situation becomes even more distressing. Methodism has deep roots in the history of early Christianity, and we need to honor this fact. It should lead us to embrace the mutual benefit of working as partners with other churches to overcome the scandal of our division.

Joint theological explorations of this and other illnesses are long overdue. And when they take place it will be important to include Africans in the exploration—something all too rare to this point. It is a well-known fact that one of the achievements of Western missions in Africa is the promotion of the study of the mother tongue. This resulted in Bibles in African languages and the beginnings of African Christian Theology.[1] There is need to continue this task of

---

1. Robert K. Aboagye-Mensah, *Mission and Democracy in Africa: the Role of the Church* (Accra: Asempa Publishers, 1994), 46-52.

African Christian theology of partnership and mutuality among African churches, but also the cooperation of the global missions boards worldwide.

Taking Ghanaian partners seriously should include engaging them in dialogue on the Eucharist. This will help reveal the deeper significance of the sacrament, and help save it from becoming an instrument of discipline and punishment or a means of exhibiting divisiveness in Christianity and in the church. It may also help us to uproot the hedges of ecclesiastical laws and disciplines that mark out distinctiveness, but prevent churches from being mutually accountable for our Christian task of evangelization. It may prevent the marginalization of the Eucharist in some Christian churches which revives the notion that it is some kind of magical rite reserved for a few.

Second on my wish list for a true ecumenicity is a better response to the challenge of multireligious living and inter-religious relations in this country and in all of Africa. In this twenty-first century of the Christian era, we need far more humility, wisdom, and openness to mutual agreement as we approach dialogue with people of other faiths. A good beginning toward this end would be to read Wesley Ariarajah's *Not Without My Neighbour*.[2] This could help us come to some common agreements and to act as partners in this regard. Ghanaian churches need to take seriously not only their unity symbolized in the Christian Council but their respect for multireligious living promoted through the Project on Christian Muslim Relations (PROCMURA). If we are to remain partners, we must respect the contexts of the other and empower their attempts to be relevant in their situations. The African scene has become most volatile, and religion is not excluded. For evangelization to become a pretext for religious wars on this continent would be a tragedy beyond measure.

A cultural and religious domination continues to exist in the relationship between the Northern churches and their Southern counterparts that thwarts any hope for mutuality and partnership. Cultural domination through education is a well-known factor, but José Chipenda, former General Secretary of the All Africa Conference of Churches (AACC), argues that "religion can be an even

---

2. Wesley Ariarajah, *Not Without My Neighbour* (Geneva: WCC, 1999).

more powerful means of control than education."[3] The relationship of the first period of evangelization of the South by the North was mostly an exercise in control. Colonial people were summoned into acquiescence. This should not be the case in this fresh millennium, for religion can be liberative if partners agree to make it so. Currently it is the tragedy of Sept 11, 2001, that fuels the focus on religion. In this setting it is vital that partners of African churches allow them to take Islam seriously and not join the bandwagon of its demonization.[4] What we need in Africa is harmonious living and not hostility toward Islam or African religion. Mutuality and manipulation cannot be bedfellows. Europeans and Ghanaians should be able to dialogue on equal terms on this challenge of our theologies of religions and of multireligious living.

Third on my wish list for partnership and mutuality in ecumenical endeavors is the manifestation of churches that truly love the world that God so loved: churches, for example, that join in partnership in facing HIV/AIDS; and churches that see respect of the sensitivities of others as our Christian duty. The hazards of life call for mutuality. It will be insufficient to address the many cultural, socioeconomic, and political challenges of our day with proposals of dogmatic solutions. This is true in Ghana as well as in the global arena. Only education will promote partnership between North and South in these death-delivering situations.

The Parallel with Men-Women Relations

The need for true partnership between Northern and Southern churches is paralleled by another challenge that we must face. Our churches need a revolution that will empower women to esteem themselves worthy to be bearers of the divine image. This revolution will require a moral resolve to position the self in a way that allows self-examination of the entitlements we take for granted. Whether we are from the North or the South, we need to face this together. Permit me to expand a bit on the partnership and mutuality in terms of men-women relations in the church, for in Africa it seems to have the lowest priority for the church—even though

3. Chipenda, "Culture and the Gospel in Changing Africa," in *The Church and the Future in Africa: Problems and Promise*, edited by Jesse Mugambi (Nairobi: AACC, 1997), 36-38.
4. Ibid., 31-32.

women are so central to the survival of church and community. This is a particularly important topic for Methodists, for we have always honored laypeople and, from the time of Susanna Wesley, have known the ministry of women. Yet, even in our midst women remain a "special issue."

I am tempted to phrase this as a question to Northern churches: Who listens to the cry of the South? Mutuality is what we need to examine and to attempt to practice, for partnership does not automatically lead to caring about what happens to the other. Mutuality, when understood, will force us to see that when one member suffers all suffer. Practical evangelism requires that human relations within the church mirror the mutual relations of the Trinity. If this happens, the world will believe us when we critique human relations in all its varieties. But too often churches refuse to treat women as equal partners with men in the mission of the church and in marriage. What is the mutual learning in relation to the challenge of the marginalization and exploitation of women in the church?

Musimbi Kanyaro challenges us with the following question: When women continue to bare their nakedness in the face of this violence, does anyone feel the shock, does the church care?[5] Over the past decade women have demonstrated mutuality and partnership through the Ecumenical Decade of Churches in Solidarity with Women, a program of the World Council of Churches. But did the churches accept that they are accountable for the lives that women live and the deaths that they die? In the church we memorialize male missionaries and conveniently forget that they were accompanied by spouses, and that many single women came as missionaries, as well. The North-South paradigm is repeated in the men-women relations. This we need to mark. It is only as partners, respecting the gifts and experiences that the other brings, that we can make statements affirming that we are one family.

Compassion

Suffering together is an important concept to examine as we seek to understand and nurture mutuality and partnership. The published

---

5. Musimbi Kanyaro, "Silenced by Culture, Sustained by Faith," in *Claiming the Promise: African Churches Speak*, edited by Margaret Larom (New York: Friendship Press, 1994), 63.

collection of the papers presented at an Ecumenical Association of Third World Theologians (EATWOT) conference held in Jos, Nigeria in 1992 contained in an appendix some letters written by the participants at the conference and used in the closing worship. A letter to Britain written by Dr. Mark Hopkins stated the following: "I know your deeds; you have a reputation of being alive, but you are dead. Wake up! Strengthen what remains and is about to die."[6] What resources of Christianity in Ghana may be harnessed for the task of reviving global Methodism? Compassion requires mutual suffering. The letter to EATWOT members written by Rev. Fr. George Ehusani cried out: "All round me there is hunger and a cry for life and for meaning. In many parts of Africa many cannot find Jesus to multiply the loaves . . . [to] free them from their chains and to heal them."[7] The cry for partnership and for mutuality is seeped through with the need for compassion. But when and how are we going to transform the tears and the protests into reconstruction of relationships between the North Atlantic and Africa? Recalling the economic exploitation of Africa by Europe, in which churches and Christians participated, Hopkins writes: "Furthermore, you have taken your wealth from the poor."[8] The question raised for partnership and mutuality is one of stewardship.

Another area of concern is how we the churches and Christians in Ghana, and the churches abroad who have accompanied us these five hundred years and more, can be one family, sharing an ethos of partnership and mutuality. This would demand a reversal of the ethos of the previous period. Once I did a research into the "Wesleyan Presence in Western Nigeria 1842–1962." Given my findings, I could not help subtitling this research "An Exploration of Power, Control, and Paternalism in Mission."[9] The paternalistic paradigm may have been unavoidable in the earlier atmosphere of Darwinian racism. However, in a globalized world we have become aware that savagery exists in all human communities, among all races, and within all classes. A dialogue of unequals is

6. Kofi Appiah-Kubi, et al., *African Dilemma: A Cry for Life* (Jos, Nigeria: EATWOT, 1992), 174.

7. Ibid., 175.

8. Ibid., 174.

9. This research was eventually published as Mercy Amba Oduyoye, *The Wesleyan Presence in Nigeria, 1842–1962: an Exploration of Power, Control, and Partnership in Mission* (Ibadan: Sefer, 1992).

inappropriate in these circumstances, just as partnership becomes a strain when viewed in terms of juniors and seniors. It is a non-starter when one declares self-sufficiency in all resources and expects nothing from the other.

As Modupe Odupoye has pointed out, we cannot easily brush over the fact that the "Basel Mission founded what became the Union Trading Company, and that the missionaries of the epoch cooperated with the European trading companies to integrate Africa into the burgeoning European capitalist international economic system."[10]

Here again the former general Secretary of AACC, Jose Chipenda, contributing to a symposium convened by AACC in 1991, called attention to "Economic Dependency and Religious Denomination." He writes: "Our dependency extends beyond a narrowly defined economic sphere. It is more evident in the realm of ideas."[11]

In this piece Chipenda argues globalization would become a positive force if it carried mutuality and partnership—for example, if Africans produced educational videos that others can use, or if they made their input into what goes on Internet, or if they were enabled to share their actualities on global networks. If Africa is empowered to be present in the family photo of the global church, we may be able to move beyond mere talk to actually practicing mutuality and partnership. There can be no partnership and mutuality when one participant has been "rendered quite impotent," says Chipenda. Partnership and mutuality require that Africa is enabled to share her alternatives to the dominant roles and voices. As it is, even the new Christian movements are failing to take Ghana's multireligious cultures seriously. With such a stance no mutuality is possible, let alone partnership in mission.

Partnership in Mission

Partnership in mission should be of special interest at this time of global religiopolitical tensions. Aaron Tolen (d. 1998), a Presbyterian from Cameroon, called for partnership to be developed first among Africans themselves; for he says "the only way out

10. Modupe Oduyoye, "Churches for Everybody," in Larom, *Claiming the Promise*, 6.
11. Chipenda, "Culture and the Gospel," 36.

of the crises seems to first be a collective struggle . . . to shape their own destiny and to make full use of their own resources without foreign intervention."[12] With intensive globalization, however, the last part of the suggestion has proved to be unrealistic, in terms of both church politics and economics. Yet this does not deny the fact that mutuality and partnership among African nations and churches is a desirable vision.

The coming into being of the African Union and the expressions of a vision of working together may be a response to prayers. Foreign funds continue to breed dependency even in the structures of the churches, making leaders cautious to speak their minds to mission partners. This remains so because Northern partners have stayed in the charity mode, not seeing the mission in Africa as properly theirs as well. The begging stance, though painful, remains with the Africans. Tolen's speech was to a WCC consolation held in Cameroon,[13] and was quoted by Nicole Fisher in "Christian Councils in the Twenty-first Century." The speech raised a number of questions that we must examine.

One of these questions is "What is the meaning of partnership in a state of dependency?" This remains a necessary question, for it was the continued presence of paternalism after we had declared partnership and mutuality in a global mission, that led to the call for a moratorium on missionary funds and personnel by some African church leaders—notably the Reverend John Gatu of Kenya, a Presbyterian. At the World Mission Conference, Bangkok 1973, and at the Third Assembly of AACC, Lusaka 1974, controversy raged over the proposed moratorium between African churches and those of the North Atlantic. The North rejected the call and accused the churches and individual Christians in Africa of wanting to withdraw from the universal church, thereby depriving the Christians of the North Atlantic and the world at large of the African contribution to the world church. What is this contribution, the role of junior partners and beggars? Moratorium became both a threat and a challenge to churches in both hemispheres. The North needed a mission field, and the South craved mission resources.[14]

---

12. Aaron Tolen, cited in Nicole Fischer, "Christian Councils in the Twenty-first Century," in Mugambi, *Church and the Future*, 202.

13. Ibid., 191.

14. Compare Jesse Mugambi, ed., *Democracy and Development in Africa: The Role of Churches* (Nairobi: AACC, 1997), 24-25.

So, the question remains: how do the two get together without the rejected paternalism? What does the North need that the South has? In the world of trade this is clear, but is it so clear in the area of spirituality? The challenge to churches in Africa becomes, "What is the African contribution to the North?" More particularly, "Does Methodism in Ghana have anything to offer to global Methodism?"

Let me offer one final image to sum up: In the first two chapters of *The African Cry*, Jean Marc Ela, a Roman Catholic from Cameroon, expounds on the issues we have been considering regarding partnership and mutuality, compassion and accountability, in the incarnation of Christianity in Africa. In the first chapter he asks whether Eucharist functions in the African churches as a symbol of salvation or dependence. In the second chapter he discusses the ambiguities of mission as these are revealed in the case of Africa. His summary judgment in this second chapter is particularly relevant to our discussion on partnership and mutuality: "Mission appears as the activity by which the church seeks to render itself unassailable. Christian universalism did not escape the ambiguities of nationalism and of colonial expansion in Africa."[15]

The surest way to avoid mutuality and partnership is to continue to refer to Africans as "the most abject creature that breathes."[16] By contrast, the beginning of mutuality and partnership is to accept that "This mission quest must not be motivated by condescension and pity."[17]

Methodism in Mission

At the roots of Methodism is open-air preaching. To this the Methodist Church in Ghana has added the gospel practice of healing and deliverance of individuals from the powers of evil. To be even more radical, we have to face squarely the social evils of our day—as the first Wesleyans did. These evils are legion and need not be discussed here. The real question is whether the churches are willing to embark on social critique and action. At the roots of Methodism is the radical notion that the church has the responsi-

15. Jean Marc Ela, *The African Cry* (Maryknoll, N.Y.: Orbis Books, 1980), 16.
16. Aboagye-Mensah, *Mission and Democracy in Africa*, 45.
17. Ela, *The African Cry*, 26.

bility to guide individuals in matters of financial management and to make them responsible for the support of the church, its ministers, and its ministry. The location of open-air preaching today includes the public media, especially television, and the churches have been in a position to buy time and to use that time responsibly.

It is not difficult to join the bandwagon of those calling for justice and compassion for children and women, the unemployed, the abused, and those living with physical and mental challenges. It is not too difficult to join the bandwagon of those who denounce corruption, abuse of power and position, and the promotion of militarism and other forms of violence in the human community. It is not difficult to pray for all sorts of people and conditions. The real challenge is to embark on *practical work* as our witness to the good news that means fullness of life for all. This, for me, is the task of being a radical Methodist today, wherever you might live and serve.

CHAPTER 11

INTERLIVING THEOLOGY AS A WESLEYAN *MINJUNG* THEOLOGY

JONG CHUN PARK

Interliving theology critically and creatively correlates the *minjung* discourse of resolving *han* for interliving with the Christian, Wesleyan discourse of faith working through love.[1] Christian discourse without *minjung* discourse will be devoid of its kerygmatic and evangelical truthfulness and will fall into a neo-colonial, egoistic spirituality. And *minjung* discourse without Christian discourse will lose its prophetic and messianic passion, only to become another odd mystery religion. That is the problem of Orientalism involved with doing theology in East Asia as well as in the rest of Asia.

A Wesleyan *minjung* theology, first of all, needs to keep its post-colonial sensibility by which it can critically examine the functioning of Christianity as a colonial ideology. It also needs to construct a genuinely ecumenical and East Asian theology that can envision both the transformation of the world of interkilling and the new

---

1. *Minjung* means common people, downtrodden and oppressed, yet also the subjects of history when they are awakened. *Han* is the feeling and experience of the suffering *minjung*. For a more detailed explanation see part 2, chapter 6, of this book.

creation of the world of interliving. Interliving theology as a Wesleyan *minjung* theology is required to take into account its Wesleyan evangelical heritage of the productive power of the Spirit of Jesus Christ on the one hand, and its noetic praxis in terms of the anamnetic solidarity with the spirits of suffering *minjung* on the other.

Critical Correlation in Interliving Theology

The core experience and language of the *minjung* is not only the context of theology but a living resource combined with the Christian Wesleyan resource. For the last several decades Asian Christian ecumenical theology has been in dialogue with other religious traditions in Asia. From the perspective of a Wesleyan *minjung* theology, we should claim that theological dialogue only with the so-called great religions (Buddhism, Confucianism, Taoism, and others) cannot but neglect the visions of the *minjung*, that is, indigenous peoples, those whom Western Christians, as well as westernized Asians, often called primitive peoples.

As Western Christian theology has fallen into logocentrism ever since it began to appropriate Greek philosophy, at the cost of destroying all "pagan" traditions, Asian theology may face a similar pitfall in encountering the classical traditions of Asian religion. But the great religions in Asia, which are certainly authentic expressions of the sacred for many Asians, cannot fully represent the *han* of the suffering *minjung*. Thus a Wesleyan *minjung* theology must incorporate, through its postcolonial critique, the stories of the suffering, surviving, and liberating *minjung*. Such postcolonial critique can be carried out in a form of priestly inscription of the *minjung*'s unjustifiable suffering, *han*, and deaths that are neither magical nor beautiful.

A Wesleyan *minjung* theology of the cross (or a cruciform inter-living theology) is necessary for overcoming the false reconciliation resulting even from the best hermeneutical correlation between the Christian classical tradition and the sacred texts of Asian religion. The Spiritual Presence in opposition to the tragic absence of the Spirit in the fractured spirits of victims and sufferers is as false as the Spirit devoid of the cross of Jesus Christ. Despite the differend (or untranslatability)[2] of the painful absence of the Spirit in the anguished spirits of the dominated, interliving theology does seek the graceful presence of the Spirit of the triune God in the brilliant darkness of *han* in the *minjung.*

Saint John of the Cross knew something about the dark night of the soul—which is not necessarily dark but sometimes brightly shining, even dazzling! And Van Gogh's painting of the starry night certainly opens up the depth of the brightly shining dark-night reality, which is contrasted with the shallowness of daylight. In the Korean minjung tradition of vocal music the shadow effect has been very important. The shadow side of the Korean *minjung*'s consciousness is identified as *han.*

Han should not be confused with resentment. *Han* cannot be overcome by taking revenge against one's enemy. Vengeance is merely a shortcut to let out *han.* To deal artfully and virtuously with *han* is to tame it by taking a long detour of practice and patience. It is the fermenting of *han.* The singer who lacks the fermented *han* cannot appeal to the souls of his or her audience. Out of the process of fermenting *han* an artist acquires more than the virtuosity of music. Out of the brilliant, dazzling darkness one reaches to the point of *"sin-myung"* (divine light in literal sense, or divine presence exuberant with joy overflowing from the guts of the soul) that resonates with the hearts of the *han*-ridden *minjung* seeking consolation and courage to survive and struggle.

Therefore, it is important to note that the two motifs of the Korean *minjung* culture, including mask dance, shamanic ritual, and pan-sori (traditional opera), are *han* and *sin-myung.* It is well known in *minjung* theology that the motif of *han* is the cluster of *minjung* experience. Without the motif of *sin-myung* there could be no soteriology in *minjung* theology. *Sin-myung* is that burst of energy that allows the crippled to dance and that springs out through the dance. Without it, the dance would be a dance of compulsion.

---

2. The differend (*différence* in French) is a term used by Lyotard. Unlike a litigation, a differend would be the case of a conflict between (at least) two parties, which cannot be equitably decided because there is no rule of judgment which can be applied to both arguments. See Jean-Francois Lyorard, *The Differend: Phrases in Dispute,* trans. Georges Van Den Abbeele (Minneapolis: University of Minnesota Press, 1999), 9-13. Postcolonial critic Gayatri C. Spivak understands the differend in terms of untranslatability of the discourse of the subaltern into that of the imperialists. See Padmini Mongia, ed., *Contemporary Postcolonial Theory: A Reader* (New York: Oxford University Press, 1997), 128.

Sin-myung is the enhanced activity of the life force that creates, liberates, and unites the life of the *minjung*. It is the mysterious fulfillment of life energy that transforms all forces of interkilling and liberates life toward a newer and greater form of interliving.

As Christians are obliged by the Spirit of Jesus Christ to witness to the gospel, Asian Christians must be ready to testify how the Spirit of Jesus Christ and the spirits of the suffering *minjung* could concur in the present state of Asian Christian faith-praxis. The testimony of the core experience and language of the *minjung* is a matter of anamnetic solidarity with the unjustifiable suffering as well as with the liberating experience of the *minjung*. We also have to consider that Christians are not necessarily the *minjung* and that becoming Christian means being witnessed by the Spirit before the person becomes a witness.

Therefore, we aim at the critical correlation between the *minjung* discourse and the Christian discourse. In a Wesleyan *minjung* theological sense we can claim that the Spirit of Jesus Christ precedes our spirits to witness for the anamnetic solidarity with the suffering and liberating experience of the *minjung*. This critical correlation of interliving theology is a kind of theological choreography that can guide Asian Christians to dance not in a geometrical equilibrium but in a dynamic balance between their Christian Wesleyan tradition and their Asian *minjung* heritage.

The Minjung *Discourse of Resolving* Han *for Interliving*

Chi-ha Kim, a famous poet in Korea, has greatly contributed to the contemporary understanding of the *minjung* religious traditions. In the beginning of the 1980s he went through a paradigmatic change in his thought and life, a change similar to conversion, from an outspoken prophetic critic against the authoritarian military regime to an outgoing, passionate preacher for the holistic liberation of life. After his long-suffering and struggling experience (he was imprisoned for more than seven years and suffered psychological illness even after he left prison), Kim encountered the core experience and language of the Korean *minjung* in and through such *minjung* religious leaders of the nineteenth century as Je-woo Choe, Si-hyung Choe, and Chung-san Kang. He witnessed on his experience in a public lecture:

> I am shipwrecked person, a street man devoid of beauty or majesty to attract others. I am neither a man of uprightness nor a thinker. I am only aware, as master Su Un (Je-woo Choe) and master Hae Wall (Si-hyung Choe) taught me, my ruined life, my soul torn apart into pieces is the very life of cosmos living in myself. I only believe that this awareness will eventually bring my salvation; thus if this awareness catches fire and gets started, my own rich yet negative experience of sin and darkness and of being killed will be dynamically transformed into the passion of new life, new creation, and new being.[3]

Chi-ha Kim once considered himself a priest of *han*. Defining *han* as "the *minjung*'s anger and sad sentiment turned inward, hardened, and stuck to their hearts," he also points out that "*han* is caused as one's outgoingness is blocked and pressed for an extended period of time by external oppression and exploitation."[4] *Han* is a psychological metaphor implying an ontological reality. *Han* is a feeling of unredeemed anguish and unresolved resentment against unjustifiable suffering. This feeling, however, is more than an individual feeling of repression. The *minjung*'s *han* in particular points beyond the psychological surface to the ontological depth of the inexhaustible suffering into which the "root chi"[5] of the *minjung*, who have been incessantly repressed and abused by the heteronomous forces of history, has turned.

The aforementioned *minjung* religious leaders lived at the end of the nineteenth century, when the Korean as well as other Asian *minjung* were under a double oppression—namely, under domestic oppression and colonial exploitation. It was Je-woo Choe who first came to an enormous conversion experience in 1860. He witnessed the "supreme *chi*" of God come upon him, and he realized that he was one with God, whom he must serve as his heavenly parents. His archetypical experience of liberation is well summarized in a mantra of 21 Chinese characters:

---

3. Chi-ha Kim, *From Burning Thirst to the Sea of Life* (Seoul: Tong Kwang Press, 1991), 36.

4. Quoted in Andrew Sung Park, *The Wounded Heart of God* (Nashville: Abingdon Press, 1993), 15.

5. Root *chi* means the primordial spirit, energy, and power. For a more detailed explanation of *chi*, see pp. 174-75 of this article.

Supreme *chi* being here and now *(ji chi keum ji)*
I yearn for its great descent *(won wi dae kang)*
God within me *(si chun ju)*
My heart in great peace *(cho wha jung)*
May forever never be forgotten *(yung se bul mang)*
To know everything *(man sa ji)*.[6]

For the first three decades after Je-woo Choe's awakening, a great number of the illiterate *minjung* joined his movement called "Donghak" (Eastern Learning) to withstand the elements of "Suhhak" (Western Learning) associated with colonialist Christianity represented at that time by Roman Catholicism. Theodore Jennings has described this movement well:

At the same time the elements of a kind of "folk Christianity" disseminated through the publication of tracts like the Gospel of Mark by clandestine Protestant missionaries were appropriated by the Donghak movement. The religious movement became in time the Donghak rebellion (1894) against concrete structures of oppression, especially the corruption whereby the ruling class *(yangban)* oppressed the *minjung*. Essential to this movement was the insistence that heaven and earth meet in the concrete presence of the other person. The other person was to be seen as the bearer of heaven or God *(si chun ju)*. As such the obeisance rendered to the divine (or by the *minjung* to the *yangban* and especially the king) was to be rendered to every person *(sa in yo chun* or "treat people as though they were God"). And this concretely meant the practice of obeisance to persons of the underclass including women, children and slaves which had been unheard of in the Confucian regime for the last half millennium. The recognition of the other as the bearer of the divine had revolutionary potential and in fact issued in revolution and remains till today as the historical irruption of the *minjung* as the subject[s] of history.[7]

The first peace movement for independence in the history of the two thirds world was launched by both Donghak and the Korean Protestant Church on 1 March 1919.

---

6. Compare *The Scripture of Chundokyo* (Seoul: Chundokyo Center, 1988).

7. Theodore W. Jennings Jr., "Transcendence, Justice, and Mercy: Toward a (Wesleyan) Reconceptualization of God," in *Rethinking Wesley's Theology for Contemporary Methodism*, ed. Randy L. Maddox (Nashville: Abingdon Press, 1998), 75-76.

What made Je-woo Choe and his followers exclaim that "the vicious cycle of the unjustifiable *han* is overcome here and now?" It was their unique experience and language of "God within me" *(si chun ju)*. Every person and even every living being, according to Si-hyung Choe (Je-woo Choe's successor), is a "God-within" being. The uniqueness of human beings is that they have to be awakened to this truth. Unless the supreme *chi* of God comes down into one's heart, there can be no awakening to God-within-ness. As in the Christian Eucharist, the invocation of the Spirit is crucial for the awakening of the Spiritual Presence. One can witness his or her being with God only after his or her being is witnessed to by God.

Wesleyan Interpretation of the Minjung Discourse

The dynamic structure of "God within-ness" *(si chun ju)* consists of two parts: one is *"si"* (within-ness or bearing) code and the other *"chun ju"* (Heavenly Lord or God) code. If we approach the *si* code from the perspective of John Wesley's "altogether a Christian," the indigenization of the Spirit of Jesus Christ in the core experience and language of the *minjung* may become fruitful. The one who is "altogether a Christian" has the witness in his or her heart on the one hand, and his or her faith works through love on the other.

The witness is the witness of the Spirit of Jesus Christ to the spirit of the Christian. It is in the first letter of John that a nearly complete internalization of witness is found: "Those who believe in the Son of God have the testimony in their hearts. Those who do not believe in God have made him a liar by not believing in the testimony that God has given concerning his Son" (1 John 5:10). Paul also exclaims: "The Spirit itself witnesses with our spirits that we are the children of God" (Rom. 8:16). Nevertheless, in the New Testament the extreme internalization of the witness is always checked and balanced by the eschatological proviso of cosmic trial. Paul Ricouer describes it well in his hermeneutic of testimony: "The Christ is witness par excellence because he evokes the 'crisis,' the judgment on the works of the world; 'I testify of it that its works are evil' (John 7:7). The function of the witness rises to the level of that of Judge of the End."[8]

---

8. Paul Ricoeur, *Essays on Biblical Interpretation* (Philadelphia: Fortress Press, 1980), 141.

Far too long the dialectic of internal witness and cosmic trial has been overlooked by the Wesleyan theology of the center. It is time to critically restore the Wesleyan eschatological proviso in order to revise, from the *minjung* perspective of the margin, the individualized form of Methodist soteriology. Wesley writes in his sermon on "The Great Assize": "All their sufferings likewise for the name of Jesus and for their testimony of a good conscience will be displayed, unto their praise from the righteous judge, their honor before saints and angels, and the increase of that far more exceeding and eternal weight of glory."[9] From the Lord's day on forever, however, the "dreadful sentence of condemnation upon those on the left" will remain "unmovable as the throne of God."[10] Wesley's vivid sense of Christian life as lived under God's constant judgment and oriented toward God's final judgment leads him to interpret the eschatological dialectic of internal witness and cosmic trial in terms of the soteriological dialectic of the spirit of bondage and the Spirit of adoption (Rom. 8:15). The spirit of bondage refers to the spiritual state under the law of sin and death. Wesley describes the state of a wounded spirit under the law: "Sometimes it may approach to the very brink of despair; so that he who trembles at the name of death may yet be ready to plunge into it every moment, to 'choose strangling rather than life' (Job 7:15)."[11] However, the one who receives the Spirit of adoption is under grace; that is, he has the power of the Holy Spirit, whereby she cries, "Abba, Father" (Rom. 8:15).

The famous Wesleyan doctrine of assurance in relation to the witness of the Spirit tends to become enthusiastic if it is disconnected from another Wesleyan doctrine, that of faith working through love. No wonder that Wesley himself changed his initial argument for assurance in the later stage of his theology. The Spirit of adoption is in other words the Love of God shed abroad in our hearts (Rom. 5:5). Wesley emphasizes the ontological priority of the Love of God over our love of God and of neighbors. The Love of God passionately urges us to love God and our neighbors. The witness of the Spirit that we are the children of God leads us into the dynamic praxis of faith working through love. As the Spirit

---

9. Sermon 15, "The Great Assize," §II.8, *Works* 1:363-64.
10. Ibid., §II.12, *Works* 1:366.
11. Sermon 9, "The Spirit of Bondage and Adoption," §II.6, *Works* 1:257.

witnesses to our spirits, the Love of God precedes our love of God and neighbors. There is a concurrence of the Spirit and our spirits, and of the Love of God and the faith that works by love. And there is a dual process of faith working through love; that is, internal witness, which is the seal of conviction that we are the children of God on the one hand, and the outward testimony of works that "is moulded on the Passion of Christ, the testimony of suffering" on the other.[12] The Wesleyan doctrine of sanctification and Christian perfection resides in a kind of Christo-praxis of faith working through love in the sense that we have the mind that Christ had and that we walk as Christ walked.

In her significant study of the book of Revelation, Elisabeth Fiorenza Schüssler reminds us of "the eschatological reservation against a spiritualistic-enthusiastic understanding of redemption and salvation." According to the theology of redemption as liberation in Revelation, "only those who, like Christ, were faithful witnesses and have been victorious in the struggle with the Roman Empire will have a part in the eschatological kingship and priesthood."[13] Wesley's concrete critique of and constant struggle against the system of capitalism has to be retained in our critique of and struggle against the "Roman Empire" in this globalized age. The Wesleyan alternative for the world of interkilling is derived from his discourse of faith that works by love. Note that Wesley developed his discourse in the eschatological context, as his sermon on "The Wedding Garment" well explains. Once again we can confirm the dialectic of internal witness and cosmic trial:

> Is there any expression similar to this of the wedding garment to be found in the Holy Scripture? In the Revelation we find mention made of "linen white and clean, which is the righteousness of the saints". . . . Is not the plain meaning of this?—it was from the atoning blood that the very righteousness of the saints derived its value and acceptableness to God. . . . What then is that holiness which is the true wedding garment, the only qualification for glory? . . . In "Christ Jesus neither circumcision availeth anything, nor uncircumcision, but a new creation," the renewal of the soul "in the image of God wherein it was created." In "Christ

---

12. Ricoeur, *Essays on Biblical Interpretation*, 142.
13. Elisabeth Fiorenza Schüssler, *The Book of Revelation* (Minneapolis: Fortress Press, 1998), 76.

Jesus neither circumcision availeth anything nor uncircumcision," but "faith which worketh by love." . . . Such has been my judgment for these threescore years, without any material alteration. Only about fifty years ago I had a clearer view than before of justification by faith: and in this from that very hour I never varied, no not an hair's breadth. Nevertheless an ingenious man has publicly accused me of a thousand variations. I pray God not to lay this to his charge! I am now on the borders of the grave, but by the grace of God I still witness the same confession. Indeed some have supposed that when I began to declare, "By grace ye are saved through faith," I retracted what I had before maintained, "Without holiness no man shall see the Lord." But it is an entire mistake; these Scriptures well consist with each other; the meaning of the former being plainly this, "By faith we are saved from sin, made holy." The imagination that faith supersedes holiness is the marrow of antinomianism. . . . (God) cries aloud, Be holy, and be happy; happy in this world, and happy in the world to come. "Holiness becometh his house for ever!" This is the wedding garment of all that are called to the marriage of the Lamb.[14]

A Wesleyan Minjung *Interpretation of Interliving Theology*

It is significant to notice that the "*si*" code in the mantra is preceded by the seven character form of invocation: "Supreme *chi* being here and now; I yearn for its great descent" (*ji chi keum ji; won wi dae kang*). This is an invocation of the Spirit of God. As is well known in East Asia, *chi* is "a vital, dynamic, original power that permeates the entire universe, indeed, all things (macrocosmic and microcosmic), and leads to an ultimate unity."[15] Taiwanese theologian Chang Chun-shen translates the Holy Spirit with *chi*. He writes: "On both sides, *chi* or spirit belongs not only to the cosmic and natural life-world, but is also closely connected with the moral dimension of human life. And over and above this, it serves as the mysterious bridge between God and the human person."[16] According to Je-woo Choe's mantra, when supreme *chi* comes upon

14. Sermon 127, "On the Wedding Garment," §§8, 17-19, *Works* 4:143, 147-48.
15. Hans Küng and Julia Ching, *Christianity and Chinese Religions* (New York: Doubleday, 1989), 266.
16. Quoted in *Christianity and Chinese Religions*, above.

the human being, the state of *si* code appears. He interprets the *si* code as the following: "inside, divine spirit; outside, *chi* moves" *(nae yu shin ryung; oe yu chi wha).* The first part of *si* code (inside, divine spirit) points to the presence of supreme *chi* in human heart so that the creative activity of a newly born person concurs with new creation by supreme *chi.* This concurrence consists of the meaning of the second part (outside, *chi* moves).

Je-woo Choe's spiritual view of reality leads into a uniquely transpersonal understanding of God. According to *si* code, when the supreme *chi* of God comes into the human heart, it turns to "divine spirit" in humanity. This should not be confused with a pantheistic identity between supreme *chi* and human spirit. When God tells Je-woo Choe in his religious experience, "my heart is thine heart" *(oh shim juk yuh shim),* this presupposes an interrelational character of the two parts. Nevertheless, the emphasis of *si* code rests upon the mystical union of God and the human since both are nothing but "one *chi*" *(il chi).* If Je-woo Choe had stopped short at this interpretation, he would have been either a pantheist or another mystic. But he goes one step further from *si* code to *chun ju* code—which he explains as "to respect God and to serve God as if we served our own parents" *(ching gi jon yi, yuh pu mo dong sa ja ya).* Je-woo Choe's interpretation of *chun ju* code reminds us of the Confucian ethos of filial sincerity. He opens up a window of a mutually critical Christian-Confucian dialogue based on the interpersonal relationship between God our parents and the human being as God's child.

It is, however, very important not to ignore that the prior state of *"si chun ju"* (God-within-ness) is the state of *han* in which the root *chi* of the *minjung* was repressed and all beings fell into the "law of interkilling" *(sang keug ji li).*[17] Chung-san Kang, one of Je-woo Choe's most prominent followers, writes: "Since the law of interkilling has prevailed through the period of the former heaven, every human affair lacked harmony and as a consequence

---

17. Originally *"sang keug"* meant "counter-living" or "inter-opposing" in contrast with *"sang saeng"* (interliving). In the classical East Asian traditions, ranging from Confucianism to Eastern medicine, *"sang saeng* and *sang keug"* go hand in hand. It was Chung-san Kang who first critically distinguished *sang keug* as interkilling from *sang keug* as counter-living, a mere opposite of *sang saeng* in harmony. Rejecting the false harmony of *sang saeng* and *sang keug* and dreaming a new world of interliving, Kang challenged the status quo of the Confucian conformity in his times.

'resentment-*han*' *(won han)* filled the whole world. This complex of resentment-*han* has caused all the miserable disasters in the world."[18] However, when the supreme *chi* of God becomes present in one's heart and one is awakened to the internal witness of "God-within" being, the root *chi* of new life and new being gets started to bring the "new beginning of the latter heaven" *(hu chun kae buk)*. Here also operates the strong tension between internal witness (inside, divine spirit) and cosmic renewal (outside, *chi* moves). At last *han* is resolved for the new beginning of life which is called by Chung-san Kang "interliving" *(sang saeng)*: interliving of God, the world, and the human. Kang said, "This is the time of 'resolving resentment-*han*' *(hae won)*. I will resolve the resentment-*han* of the woman who has been imprisoned at home, no more than man's plaything and slave from thousands of years, in order to establish the correct relationship between yin and yang or between earth and heaven."[19]

In East Asia there has never been a time of genuine peace and justice. The Korean *minjung* has suffered Chinese domination in the old past, Japanese imperialism in the recent past, and American hegemony in the present. U.S. President George W. Bush, in his State of the Union Address (29 January 2001), described North Korea as one of the countries making up an axis of evil. Bush's remark reminds us of former U.S. President Reagan's notorious rendering of Russia as the "evil empire." This kind of political rhetoric is not free from the U.S. imperialist ideology, often disguised in the rhetoric of Christian faith. During Bush's joint visit with South Korean President Kim Dae-jung to Dorasan Station (21 February 2002), which is located in the demilitarized zone between North and South, their speeches clearly revealed the fundamental differend[20] between the U.S. hegemony and the Korean *minjung*. Kim talked about the *han* of the Korean *minjung* suffering in the only divided nation of the world. Bush once again condemned North Korea by calling it the most dangerous nation with the most dangerous weapons. Bush's rhetoric of freedom worked to divide (and to rule!) the two Koreas, the South enjoying political freedom and economic affluence under the U.S. blessing, and the North remaining a despotic

---

18. *Daesoonjeonkyung* (The Scripture of Chungsankyo), 5:4.
19. *Daesoonjeonkyung*, 5:134.
20. See footnote 2.

regime robbing freedom and prosperity from its starving people. Nevertheless, the apparent atheism of North Korean communism partly works against the fetish domination of mammon in both the U.S. and South Korea, while the apparent theism of Mr. Bush's faith, as well as that of most anti-communist South Korean Christians, actually means capitalist, imperialist, and neocolonial ideology suffocating the national autonomy of North Korea.

The world after the incidents of September 11, 2001, has increasingly revealed itself as the world of interkilling. Asia, from Palestine to Korea, has seemed to fall inescapably into final global conflict between the good, sole super power and the handful of bad terrorists as well as their supporters in the so-called axis of evil. It is indeed the problem of interkilling. It is a conflict between terrorists against the U.S. and warmongers against anti-U.S. terrorism. There is a vicious cycle of interkilling—that is, of terrorism and war. The Bush government takes its arrogant foreign policy of unilateralism for granted. It supposes and propagandizes that those who do not take sides with the U.S. war against terrorism are its enemy. It refuses to inquire into the root cause of anti-U. S. terrorism.

The arbitrary and unilateral actions of the Bush administration have heightened tensions in Korea and have raised the specter of another Korean War. The U.S. seems to prefer confrontation and interkilling to engagement and interliving. The Korean *minjung* in both North and South must have been shocked by the U.S. hardline attitude, which has dampened the expectations for a détente on the Korean peninsula that had been growing since the historic Pyongyang Summit (15 June 2000), in which the leaders of the two Koreas shook hands for the first time since Korea was divided by the U.S. and the U.S.S.R. in August 1945.

The only viable alternative for survival and interliving in Korea today is to live and let live, rephrasing Wesley's dictum "to think and let think." On 12 October 1999, William Perry, former U.S. Defense Secretary, presented his "Review of United States Policy Toward North Korea" to the Senate Foreign Relations Subcommittee. The essence of his presentation can be summarized in one sentence: "We have to deal with the North Korean Government not as we wish they would be, but as in fact they are." Unlike allies of the U.S., such as Japan, South Korea, and the

Philippines, which accept agreements that diminish their sovereignty in the interest of regional security, North Korea is not an ally of the U.S. and sovereignty is its greatest pride. We must recognize that both the U.S. and South Korea have wished, during almost a decade of unprecedented natural disasters and complete economic shambles in North Korea, that it would eventually collapse. Perry's report reflects a rare spirit of political realism not to interkill but to interlive. Such spirit of interliving was also prophetically stated by former U.S. ambassador to South Korea, James T. Laney: "The first thing that we must do to break the stalemate of the Cold War is to acknowledge the right of the other side to exist. Going beyond the Cold War means that the defeat of the other side is not the principal aim either passively by attrition or actively as in war."[21]

Conclusion

In Asia today mere religious dialogue is misleading if it is not carried out in relation to emancipation of the *minjung* and liberation of life. There is no purely religious dialogue that should be disconnected from ideological, politico-economical, and ecological matters. "A Statement of Concerns of Asian Methodist Bishops" succinctly describes the contemporary Asian situation:

> Asia, the origin of the world religion and civilization, has more than half of the 6 billion world population. Democracy, communism, monarchical governments, and military autocracy are co-existing in the continent. But, now it is suffering from the conflicts between races, religions, and castes, and is facing serious problems about human rights, environment, food, child abuse, violence on women, the gap between the rich and the poor, joblessness, disease, war, and so on and on. Especially the conflicts between races and religions could develop into serious war.[22]

Facing innumerable communal conflicts among various ethnic groups, cultures, languages, and ways of thought, Asian Christians

---

21. Compare James T. Laney, "Beyond the Cold War," 75th Anniversary Lecture and Symposium: "The Peacemaking Church," 22-23 April 1999, Seoul.

22. "A Statement of Concerns of Asian Methodist Bishops," Conference of Asian Methodist Bishops, 16-19 February 2002, Seoul.

should stand with the suffering *minjung* in order to sustain their societies in the spirit and ethos of interliving that has become imperative and a necessity. "The Spirit at Work in Asia Today," a document presented by the Federation of Asian Catholic Bishops' Conference, powerfully states:

> We value pluralism as a gift of the Spirit. There is also a situation of pluralism that results from the different ways people respond to the prompting of the Spirit, which the Asian Bishops have called "receptive pluralism." Again, people encounter the Spirit within their context, which is pluralistic in terms of religions, cultures, and world views. In this light, we affirm a stance of receptive pluralism. That is, the many ways of responding to the prompting of the Holy Spirit must be continually in conversation with one another.[23]

How could a Wesleyan *minjung* theology contribute to the world-historical paradigm change from the yang (male-dominated) culture of interkilling to the yin (feminist) culture of interliving?[24] First and foremost, interkilling theology should be deconstructed. One of the typical models for interkilling theology is the *Heilsgeschichte* model.[25] It has dominated Western (both Catholic and Protestant) theology for a long time. It has been established on the most horrible doctrine of double predestination that divides humankind into two interkilling camps, that is, the elected and the reprobate. This political-theological doctrine rules the day from Palestine (Jews versus Arabs) to Korea (Christians

---

23. Compare "The Spirit at Work in Asia Today: A Document of the Office of Theological Concerns of the Federation of Asian Catholic Bishops' Conference," 1997, Sampran.

24. The Korean *minjung* religions overthrew the age-old rule of the *I-Ching* (The Book of Change) that is based on the false harmony of yin-yang symbolism. The notion of yin came from the imagery of shadow, and it signifies femaleness, receptiveness, passivity, and coldness. The notion of yang came from the imagery of brightness, and it signifies maleness, creativity, activity, and warmth. The distortion of the yin-yang symbolism lies in the ideology of false harmony repressing and eliminating any tension and conflict between opposite sexes, races, and classes. Appropriating Il-boo Kim's Correct Change, Chung-san Kang calls the new world of interliving in terms of "correct yin and correct yang" *(chung eum, chung yang)*. For the time being, however, Kang asserts that feminist challenge against male domination is necessary. It is a strategic step toward the final goal of the genuine harmony between yin and yang.

25. The *Heilsgeschichte* (history of salvation) model falls short because of the historicist exclusivism of Christ-centeredness and loses sight of the larger context of the divine *oikonomia* for the ecumenical household of the triune God, embracing nature as well as history. Compare Konrad Raiser, *Ecumenism in Transition* (Geneva: WCC Publications, 1996), 65-71.

versus Communists) and in every corner around the globe (good people versus terrorists).

Yet, is God only the God of Abraham, Isaac, and Jacob? Is not the God of Jesus Christ also the God of Hagar, Ishmael, and Esau? Many forms of liberation theology are nothing but the bearers of *han* cries of the Hagars, Ishmaels, and Esaus in our time. Liberation theologies remind us of the theological significance of the core experience and language of the *minjung*. If the liberation model is understood to be diametrically opposed to the *Heilsgeschichte* model, could interkilling theology be overcome? Despite their apparent claim for Christian identity, some liberation theologians tend to mislead ecumenical theology as long as the Scriptures are one-sidedly considered the texts of interkilling, and the critical distinction between the spirits of the suffering creatures and the Spirit of Jesus Christ is blurred. Enter a Wesleyan *minjung* theology as interliving theology. The fundamental trait of interliving theology can be identified by its emphasis on "free grace for and in all" (John Wesley).

If we could critically and creatively correlate the Wesleyan doctrines of free grace, of assurance, and of faith working through love with the *minjung* discourse of resolving *han* for interliving in relation to its messianic vision of new being, we might come up with a new heuristic model for the interpretation of the Scriptures as the texts of interliving. And this new reading of the Scriptures would surely comply with the highest vision of Wesleyan Christian faith, that is, Universal Redemption as New Creation that has been yearned for even by the groaning creatures (Rom. 8:19-22).

CHAPTER 12

[Y]OUR BOOK, [Y]OUR READING

Writing Täsilisili *Readings*

JIONE HAVEA

Reading across and for the underside of texts is *in* these days. It is hip to transgress and shift textual limits, and undermine the powers that be, but the limits of those textual and ideological boundaries, the limits of the limits, often escape appraisal. Why should one bother with boundaries and/or powers that be that do not limit her, and have no bearing on who she is? As far as she is concerned, those are not boundaries. This essay attends to one of the boundaries, the Bible, which South Pacific islanders associate with Methodism, one of the religious movements responsible for bringing Christendom to our liquid continent.

South Pacific islanders are beginning to realize, thanks to reluctance at the grass roots, that the Bible is not an indigenous text. Whether it is a western book[1] and/or a church book[2] is not the issue here. I leave that decision for the Bible-as-book-police-force. My concern is with the fact that the Bible is not a South Pacific island book. Unlike other things introduced to our shores, like clothing

---

1. See Gary W. Trompf, *The Gospel Is Not Western: Black Theologies from the Southwest Pacific* (Maryknoll, N.Y.: Orbis, 1987).
2. See Phyllis A. Bird, *The Bible as the Church's Book* (Philadelphia: Westminster, 1982).

and metal, which our ancestors appropriated for island conditions and ways, the Bible was introduced, but not handed over. It was given but not surrendered, withheld, in between being given and being received, so that it continues to be a *gift* (Derrida) that islanders have yet to own. Islanders could not claim the Bible as "our book" because they were taught to depend on the directions of the bearers of the Bible, the people with the power of knowledge and arms, on how to handle it. The withholding of control is another reminder that the Bible is a foreign commodity.

Modern modes of reading are also foreign to our surroundings.[3] These practices are exclusivist—insofar as Westerners and Easterners have circumscribed how biblical texts are to be read, and "circumcized" dissidents, without accounting for those of us who are in between. They are also elitist—insofar as one becomes a student to be a reader. I respond to those attitudes in this essay with what unschooled, unscholarly, subjects from the South Pacific islands, in between West and East, may add to biblical interpretation.[4]

I will first introduce two companions of the Bible, the conditionings of "discovery" and "education," and then present *täsilisili* responses to two biblical events, the judgment of Solomon and the resurrection of Jesus. These responses will shift the limits of "radical Methodism" from a religious movement to a manner of reading, indicating that islanders do take the Bible seriously, while *at the same time* maintaining the "Protestant" flavor of the Methodist movement.

Whose Bible?

The Bible was introduced by Westerners who came to discover and mark new land, to civilize and normalize primitive faces, and to save savage souls. Our ancestors became "objects of the look"

---

3. See also Mary McClintock Fulkerson, *Changing the Subject: Women's Discourses and Feminist Theology* (Minneapolis: Fortress Press, 1994); Daniel Patte, *Ethics of Biblical Interpretation: A Reevaluation* (Louisville: Westminster John Knox, 1995); Rasiah S. Sugirtharajah, *Bible and the Third World: Precolonial, Colonial, and Postcolonial Encounters* (New York: Cambridge University Press, 2001); and Gerald O. West, *Academy of the Poor: Towards a Dialogical Reading of the Bible* (Sheffield: Sheffield Academic Press, 1999).

4. The "in-between-ness" of the subjects I represent in this essay is highlighted by the fact that they are migrants to Australia. They call two places home, Tonga and Australia, *as if they [do not] belong to both.* See Sugirtharajah, *Bible and the Third World*.

(the stuff of *orientalism*), and of the shot, rather than caretakers of the land they occupy.[5] The Bible was one of the tools in the expeditions of *discovery*, and natives did not distinguish discoverers and colonizers from missionaries. As objects of the look also, later settlers looked the same, clothed from top to bottom as if they are disguised and protected, carrying books and tools that spit fire (guns), give them cover (umbrellas), and so forth. They touch natives from afar with their lead-throwing sticks (guns) held together with their books. Submitting to the *arms* of later settlers also meant submitting to the books that they carried; and natives quickly learned that their own clubs and sticks were no match. In the arms of later settlers (whether discoverers, colonizers, or missionaries), therefore, the Bible came as an object of respect and fear, two overlapping responses.

And through the mouths of missionaries, the Bible turned into an instrument of judgment. It was used to teach our ancestors how they were savages who must stop being islanders if they wished to be saved from the wrath of God and the guns of settlers. This was not a clash between Bible (more appropriately, "gospel") and culture but a clash between cultures, for the Bible, too, is a cultural product. What the natives could not distinguish were the differences between Western and biblical cultures. They came together, at once, cooperating in the ventures of discovery/colonization/conversion. Their arrival marked the transformation of native cultures, the repression of some of our native identity markers. Notwithstanding, at least three qualifications are necessary here.

First, it is naive to think that the Bible, as a book, changed native cultures independently of the desires and working of its bearers. The Bible did not fire the shots, nor directly judge South Pacific island cultures. But it is also naive to imagine that the responsibility for the cultural clash rests solely on the shoulders of discoverers/colonizers/missionaries. To do so is to sidestep the political nature of the Bible.[6] Moreover, to focus on the differences between the Bible and its bearers, as if the Bible could have come without bearers,

---

5. On Aotearoa, see Jeff Evans, *The Discovery of Aotearoa* (Auckland: Reed, 1998); and David Gunn, "Colonialism and the Vagaries of Scripture," in *God in the Fray*, edited by Tod Linafelt and Timothy Beal (Minneapolis: Fortress Press, 1998), 127-42.

6. See Danna N. Fewell and David M. Gunn, *Gender, Power & Promise: The Subject of the Bible's First Story* (Nashville: Abingdon Press, 1993); and The Bible and Culture Collective, *The Postmodern Bible* (New Haven: Yale University Press, 1995).

is to avoid accounting for the significance of our cultures and the blood of our ancestors. In that regard, this essay does not seek to lay the blame on either the book or its bearers, but to give face to, to embrace the faces of, South Pacific island natives. I am, of course, biased, for native blood flows in my veins.

Second, I am not suggesting that presettlement native cultures were perfect. I am not even sure that a "perfect culture" exists. Speaking realistically, even if it is pessimistic, there will always be overlords and undersides of cultures. Furthermore, it is naive to suggest that native cultures would have remained unchanged had Westerners not landed at our shores. Cultural changes are inevitable, and possible because natives accept them; some changes may be resisted, but some are adapted and normalized. If "the look" is the spark that fires up orientalism and if "expecting natives to be different" is the fuel that keeps orientalism ablaze, then the third form of orientalism, the wind that keeps the fiery mouth of orientalism gnawing, is when natives accept the changes expected of them. In other words, our ancestors are responsible for accepting the changes that the Bible and its bearers brought, even if those cultural changes were forced upon them; but they are not responsible for the *arms* of the bearers.

Third, I should add that natives did not always fall victim to the guns of the settlers. Some of the settlers were clubbed, and their bodies boiled and eaten. Cannibalism, of course, even though it finds a place in Eucharistic talks, is savagery, and we are not proud of our ancestors' behaviors. With respect to the ideological aspect, natives gave the impression that they accepted all of the settlers' teachings, but within native circles, they talked about how, now and then, they fooled the settlers. They bowed to the arms of settlers, but they were not fully on board with them; they faked submission, partial submission.[7] Whether this behavior was resistance, reluctance, or racism is not my concern here. I only wish to point

---

7. The 1885 establishment of the *Siasi Tonga Tau'ataina* (Free Church of Tonga) manifests the complexity of partial submission. Led by King George Tupou I and Shirley Baker, who deviated from his fellow Methodist missionaries, *Siasi Tonga Tau'ataina* was formed by subjects who left the *Siasi Uesiliana* (Wesleyan Methodists). The breakage was motivated by respect to the king and in resistance to the *Siasi Uesiliana*, who came to be known as *Fakaongo* ("to listen/adhere" [to overseas leadership]). Ironically, *Siasi Tonga Tau'ataina* did not want to *fakaongo* to overseas authorities but in fact followed an overseas authority, Shirley Baker. On the other hand, *Siasi Uesiliana* did not want to *fakaongo* to the king. In other words, partial submission happened on several levels.

out that the natives of the South Pacific islands were not always *pacific,* or *pacified.* I explore this complex further in the alternative responses to Solomon's wisdom and Jesus' resurrection.

The above qualifications give a more critical and partial account of the circumstances into which the Bible was introduced, making more complex the inculturation that the arrival of the Bible affected. A more concrete example of this inculturation coincides with the concern of missionaries to educate natives. In addition to erecting places of worship and hospices, settlers built schools. These were places in which natives were taught the ways of the settlers and where native languages, our *speeches,* were put into *writing.* Natives were taught to see what they hear with their ears, to send words without a voice, and to communicate with stones and paper which appear more enduring than the smoke signals *(täsilisili)* with which they were accustomed.[8] Words became stable and at once guarded, because only those who learned to read knew what was written. Whereas *täsilisili* is open for all to read and interpret, and for change in the atmosphere, for transformation, a written message may only be read by the few who receive it. At the underside of this progress was the desire of missionaries to translate the Bible into the native languages.

I do not wish to debate the difference between *speech* and *writing.* I leave that for Jacques Derrida. Rather, I use this opportunity to push two bearings of South Pacific island/oceanic reading: the freedom involved in reading *täsilisili,* smoke signal, and the expectation that texts (smoke) are elusive, both of which were discouraged upon the establishment and institutionalization of schools and *writing.* I do not lament the transition to writing, but the discouragement of *reading writing as if it is täsilisili.* The reading of *täsilisili* was playful, creative, and imaginative, because it involved reading a flowing text, a silent text that fluctuates in its deliverance, a hazy text that escapes as it materializes. Whereas Derrida pays attention to the ashes, the cinders that remain, the South Pacific island/oceanic reader of *täsilisili* reads a text that fades, and escapes. Lacking an academic label for this mode of reading, I refer to it as *täsilisili reading,* a label that I expect to escape rigidity.

---

8. Of course, communication by smoke signals was not unique to our cultures and it has not been distinguished from our contemporary societies.

185

Because of the elusiveness of the text, *täsilisili reading* focuses on the fleeting text rather than the intention of the sender. Right versus wrong reading, the concern of "school readings," is not the primary issue in *täsilisili reading*. Rather, "right and/or wrong for whom" is the stuff of *täsilisili reading*.

There is always the chance that different *täsilisili readers* will read a text (smoke signal) differently, not just because they may see the text at different moments of its delivery, from different positions and directions, but because a text may develop into a different signal (than what the sender intended). For instance, a signal for "bring food for burial ritual" may be transformed into "come and feast" during its delivery. One text is delivered as two texts, a disseminating text, one text opens up to two readings, double readings, both of which are "right" because a burial is an event to which people both bring food and come to feast. But for the grieving family, "come and feast" means that they may not have enough food for everyone. Right or wrong text/reading for whom?

Performed on biblical texts, *täsilisili reading* embraces the playfulness and openness of those texts, and reconsiders the limits of dominant readings, of your readings. This is a sublime way of bringing "your Bible and your reading" to meet "our Bible and our reading."

Whose Reading?

What if Solomon was wrong?

When I was asked to deliver the Bible studies for the 2001 New South Wales Synod of the Uniting Church in Australia, I approached the islander inmates with whom I sit at Parklea Prison (New South Wales) to help me pick the texts and to share their readings of them.[9] One of the texts we chose was 1 Kings 3:16-28, which dominant readers take as a testimony to Solomon's wisdom. The following week, I shared with the inmates my reading of this story, which I then wrote up for my Bible study. It was something like this:

---

9. The three Bible studies are posted at the *Insights Magazine* website: http://insights.uca.org.au/2001/november/synodbiblestudies.htm (accessed 19 April 2002).

In the previous story, Solomon has a dream in which he asks for "an understanding mind" to "govern" Israel and to be "able to discern between good and evil" (3:3-9). In the same dream God accepts Solomon's request, declaring:

I now do according to your word. Indeed I give you a wise and discerning mind; no one like you has been before you and no one like you shall arise after you. I give you also what you have not asked, both riches and honor all your life; no other king shall compare with you. If you walk in my ways, keeping my statutes and my commandments, as your father David walked, then I will lengthen your life. (3:12-14)

Solomon asks for one thing, "an understanding mind," and receives three things in advance of his asking: unmatchable status, riches and honor, and the chance for a long life. The saying "be careful what you ask for, because you might get it" does not explain Solomon's situation. He gets more than he asked for! This exchange takes place in a dream (3:5, 15), the realm of desire and the subconscious (Freud, Lacan). Upon awaking Solomon returns to Jerusalem where he encounters two mothers in the realm of consciousness.

The two women are said to be prostitutes who live in the same house, with no one else, male or female, family member or patron.[10] In three days time the house of two women grows to four persons, two mothers and a son each. Then death visits the house that has thus far been filled with cries of birth and life. One of the sons dies one night, but we are not told how old he was. The mothers are still nursing their sons and we are told that the child dies because, as one woman charges, his mother lay on him. In this story, neither the mothers nor their sons are named.

The women come to the king endowed with the ability to "discern between good and evil." One woman accuses the other mother of switching their sons in the middle of the

---

10. There are many gaps in this story—for example, we are not told who or where the fathers lived—which I will ignore in this reading. Suffice it to say that such gaps add to the prostitutizing of the mothers, from whose house the fathers of their sons are removed.

night—she allegedly took her dead son and laid him at the breast of the accuser, then took the accuser's living son and laid him at her own breast. When the accuser awoke the next morning to nurse her son, she looked closely and saw that the child at her side was clearly not her son.

The two women argue before the king, who orders that a sword be brought to divide the living child in two, a half for each mother. Solomon sounds very much like Judah in Genesis 38, quickly passing the judgment of death. Whereas elders usually decide with lots, which are not physically harmful, Solomon calls for a sword. He calls for division to give death to the living child and motherlessness to both women, to give death and division. I cannot tell if Solomon is serious or bluffing, but I cannot applaud his mandate out of fear that he was serious. Nor do I accept his mandate as wise, out of respect for the ability of mothers to recognize the children they bore. I assume that a mother, no matter how old her child is, whether one day old or older, would know what her son looks like. I assume also that she would know her child by a name.

I assume that the king's mandate would have been carried out had not the mother of the living child—because compassion for her son burned within her—told the king not to kill the boy, but to give him to the other woman. "Please, my lord, give her the living boy; certainly do not kill him!" Her plea brings two reactions. The other mother says, "It shall be neither mine nor yours; divide it!"[11] And the wise king changes his mind: "Give the first woman the living boy; do not kill him. She is his mother" (3:26-27).

A mother echoes the division that the king proposed, and the king upholds her wish by declaring the other woman as the mother of the living child. And Israel "stood in awe of the king, because they perceived that the wisdom of God was in him, to execute justice" (3:28). Israel fails to see that the strife between the women helped Solomon's judgment; nor does Israel recognize that Solomon's "justice" drives the women apart. We do not know what

---

11. NRSV dehumanizes the child, kills the child in advance, by referring to him as "it."

happened after Solomon's judgment, whether the women continued to live together in the same house, whether the dead child
received an honorable burial, and so forth. The mothers exit as
"mother of dead boy" and "mother of living boy," one carrying a
child; in other words, Solomon's justice solidifies the division
between two women who live in the same house.

In response to my reading, one of the inmates, Sione
Tonga'onevai, asked, "What if Solomon was wrong?" It was
because of his *täsilisili* move that I ended my Bible study for the
Synod by deconstructing my own reading. I closed with
Tonga'onevai's *täsilisili* query: What if it was the mother of the
dead child who said, "Please, my lord, give her the living boy . . .
do not kill him"?[12] *What if* the mother of the dead child has seen
enough death for one day and did not want Solomon to bring his
sword upon another child?[13] She wanted a living child, not a dead
one, and why do we not give her a chance to be a loving mother?

In this *täsilisili reading*, I resist the temptation to endorse the
king's word in order to *release* the possibility that both mothers
want to hold a living child. I do not look on the women as if only
one is right so the other must be wrong; I do not read with
Solomon's wisdom. Insofar as a *täsilisili reading* is not concerned
about right and/or wrong reading, but for whom is it right and/or
wrong, the foregoing resists siding with one or the other woman,
opting to be on both sides. I raise the possibility that both women
could be right, which means that both could be wrong, and I
trust that they have already forgiven my *täsilisili reading!* This first
example of *täsilisili reading* calls upon readers to account *for whom*
they read.

Why didn't Jesus appear to Pilate after he rose from the dead?

The second example of a *täsilisili reading* comes from another
unscholarly context, a gathering of ordinary Tongan kava drinkers

---

12. Both women are nameless in the story, so it is difficult to tell which woman was doing
and saying what.

13. It is reasonable to imagine that it was the mother of the living child who answered "It
shall be neither mine nor yours; divide it!" On the one hand, getting rid of the child will give
her more time and freedom to do her work as a prostitute. On the other hand, she offers to
share her child with her housemate. A third reading is also possible: she was calling
Solomon's bluff. None of these readings is comforting, but they are possible.

called *Föfö'anga* ("pumice"), a practice that has drifted to several countries. In Australia, members of *Föfö'anga* formed a *Pakipaki folofola* fellowship (*pakipaki* is the Tongan word for "breaking," as in "breaking bread," and *folofola* stands for "Scripture"), a gathering that is deconstructive in name and by practice. The *Pakipaki folofola* fellowship at Strathfield (New South Wales) goes by another name, *Fakatu'amelie* ("sweet expectation"), as if "breaking Scripture" will materialize sweet expectations.[14] It is with this group that I sit and reflect on lectionary readings most Wednesday evenings.

On the Wednesday of Holy Week 2002, the conversation circled around the story of the resurrection. Since Tongans have deep respect for the dead, past and present, and often speak of (visiting) the realms of the spirits, the claim that Jesus rose from the dead was not problematic for the group. Rather, our focus was on the events that took place after the resurrection. During the conversation Sione Taulahi raised a silly but very critical question: *Why didn't Jesus appear to Pilate after he rose from the dead?* It is silly because Bible readers are sure that Jesus did not appear to Pilate, and it is speculative to consider such "why" questions. "Why don't you phone him and ask?" was one of the initial responses offered! Upon further reflection, the group wondered if all of the post-resurrection events were recorded in the Gospels.[15] If not, as with the life of Jesus, then it is possible that Jesus appeared to Pilate but the Gospel writers did not bother to inquire about it nor record it. The Gospels, after all, are Christian, not Roman, literature. They are biased against Roman views and faces. On the other hand, it would not be of benefit for Pilate to bear witness to the resurrection of Jesus. The possibilities disseminate! Suddenly the "silly" (same pronunciation as for *sili* in *tä-sili-sili*) question produces a "smart" reading, *breaking scriptures* in the process. It exposes the political nature of Gospel narratives, and expresses a longing for the faces and views of the ousted (Pilate).

Things would have been less problematic had Jesus done what the foregoing *täsilisili reading* prefers. In the first place, followers would not have had such a difficult time explaining the resurrection. And since in *täsilisili* circles it is easier to convince an outsider

---

14. This echoes the alternative name for a similar fellowship in Tonga, *Fakalelu* ("comfort"), which implies that comfort is attained when Scripture is broken.

15. Mark's two endings, highlighted in the Tongan translation, invites a "third ending," in which a *täsilisili reader* may insert an appearance to Pilate!

than an insider, it may have been easier for Jesus to convince Pilate that he has risen from the dead (cf. John 20). In the second place, there may have been better relations between "Christians" and "non-Christian Romans" in the early church. And in the third place, readers of Revelation, for example, would not have reached absolute readings that the "great whore" in chapters 17 and 19 refers only to the Roman Empire. Who knows, maybe the Bible would not have ended with such a judgmental book as Revelation.

This *täsilisili reading* is not concerned with what actually happened, but how things could have been easier *(for whom?)* had Jesus appeared to Pilate. At the underside of this reading is the sublime suggestion that Jesus could have done things differently, that the *Pakipaki folofola* fellowship could have done things more effectively. It is a "wrong" reading by "school" standards, but empowering for ordinary subjects who experience the *pleasure of reading* in "breaking Scripture." It is for this kind of reading that I push in this reflection on "radical Methodism."

If *täsilisili reading* is allowed to be "radical" in the proceedings of contemporary "Methodism," it will be, to borrow a line from Mark Joffe's *The Man who Sued God*, "a great victory for ordinary people."[16]

Whose *täsilisili* reading?

The manner of reading that I have sketched will not be appropriate for all natives of the South Pacific and Oceania. It is not in the interest of natives to make universal and global claims. I leave that for readers who bank on globalization.

On the other hand, this manner of reading just may be "island stuff," *lölenga fakamotu*, limited and limiting. So be it! It is not in the interest of islanders to be defensive either, but to *pakipaki* ("break") further. With this privilege, which was withheld at the arrival of the Bible, natives may come to see how the Bible is also *our* book. In other words, "breaking Scripture" is the stuff of responsibility, of response-ability (Levinas), of *responding to writing as if it is täsilisili.*

Finally, "What if . . . " and "Why didn't . . . " are not wishful questions, even if they are speculative, but the stuff of responsibility. Such are the kinds of questions that natives in the mission fields would like later settlers to address.

---

16. Mark Joffe, director, *The Man Who Sued God* (Australian Film Financing Commission, New South Wales Film and Television Office, Showtime Australia, 2001).

CHAPTER 13

METHODISM AND LATIN AMERICAN LIBERATION MOVEMENTS

JOSÉ MÍGUEZ BONINO

Latin American so-called liberation theologians have always insisted that "liberation" be understood as "a road to freedom." Freedom in the full sense and scope of the word is the goal and the promise toward which any legitimate liberation movement intends to move and which, therefore, has to shape its immediate goals and actions. Consequently, liberation movements always have a certain "relativity"—they intend to attain specific achievements which are certainly limited and temporary but which, at the same time, point to, and in some measure anticipate, the full freedom which in Christian terms we symbolize as the kingdom of God, the New Jerusalem, the perfect Shalom. In this tension between achievement and promise, liberation movements are always at risk either of idolizing the immediate goals and thus becoming "reactionary," or of defusing their action into utopian dreams and thus becoming useless and, in another way, also reactionary.[1] More specifically, "liberation"

---

1. This tension is recognized and discussed in the first two "classics" in Latin American Liberation Theology: Gustavo Gutiérrez, *A Theology of Liberation* (Maryknoll, N.Y.: Orbis Books, 1973) (first edition in Spanish as *Teología de la liberación*, 1971); and Rubem A. Alves, *A Theology of Human Hope* (Washington: Corpus Books, 1969).

has been classically used to refer to social and political conditions—for instance, as "liberation from slavery" or from "foreign domination"—although it has also personal, cultural, and religious dimensions: gender, sin, demonic powers, psychological disturbances, taboos, and so on. In this consideration of "liberation movements" in Latin America I will focus on the social, economic, and political dimensions of oppression and liberation, although I recognize that other factors are also present and have to be recognized and taken into account.

The notion of liberation has "oppression" as an unavoidable correlate. Any movement for liberation at the economic, political, or social level is determined by the existence of concrete and specific forms of oppression and individual or collective agents of oppression. Whether or not these agents are aware of their responsibility, whether they see the situation as natural and unavoidable, or assume it as a conscious and voluntary cause (whatever may be their way to justify it) may change the way in which the oppressed interpret the nature and means needed to achieve their liberation, but cannot do away with the antitheses between liberation and oppression and, eventually, the confrontation of oppressed and oppressors. However, the assessment of these different conditions is decisive for the means and the processes of liberation.

It is also important to recognize the fact that while oppression may appear *dominantly* as economic exploitation, or racial discrimination, or political domination, and so on, the other dimensions are also normally put at the service of this dominant organizer of oppression. If we are not aware of these relations, a movement for liberation which "reduces" its efforts to one single factor—even if it is the dominant one—runs the risk of alienating those who feel oppression at ano-ther level and offers the oppressor a way of using the contradictions of the different victims of oppression to neutralize their efforts.

Oppression and Liberation in Latin America

Different forms of social, ethnic, economic, and political oppression had existed in these lands that we now call Latin America long before the arrival of the European conquerors. Aboriginal tribes and nations were subdued by invading peoples and subjected to different forms of oppression. The Inca and the Aztec empires are perhaps the best known but not the only examples. Studies developed in the last half century have contributed to a much more detailed and realistic picture of the preconquest conditions of the indigenous populations, and at the same time, to a recognition of the diversity of situations and a critique of the myths of "the semi-human" and of the "noble savage."

The arrival of the European conquerors, however, opened a totally new chapter in the history of the original populations of the continent. It was a prolonged, total, radical, and brutal appropriation of the land, the resources, and the political, economic, cultural, and religious control of the continent. The story is vastly documented and we do not need to enter into the discussion of the different, and sometimes contradictory, interpretations. Whether we call it decimation, exploitation, civilization, or evangelization of these peoples, there is no way to deny that it was an attempt at a total "appropriation" and, therefore, whatever the intentions, a total control of the lives of these people, in other words, *oppression.* An "attempt," I say, because it did not go without resistance. There were indigenous revolts that reappeared here and there even centuries after the arrival of the conquerors. There was a passive resistance that kept hold of old traditions, religious beliefs, music and dance, and myths and legends—sometimes behind the back of the "conquistadores," other times craftily hidden or wisely amalgamated with those of the invaders. Should not we recognize these facts as "liberation movements" coming from the people and their native leadership? But there were also liberation movements that originated in the conscience of persons and groups of the conquerors. The most significant were, without doubt, the well-known protests and projects of the religious leadership (particularly in some of the religious orders) that we usually identify with the name of Bartolomé de las Casas. This was not a solitary effort; it involved a number of initiatives which included a direct relation with the "oppressed" and a task of conscientization and theological, juridical, and political pressure on the conqueror.[2] Interestingly

---

2. In a carefully documented work, Gustavo Gutiérrez has produced the best account of this movement, its origins, conditions, achievements, and weaknesses: *Las Casas: In Search of the Poor of Jesus Christ: Evangelization and Theology in the Sixteenth Century* (Maryknoll, N.Y.: Orbis Books, 1993).

enough, although John Wesley does not seem to be very aware of the Latin American world, when he comes to think of "oppressed people," he starts by mentioning the "thousands, myriads, if not millions" of Africans "driven to market and sold like cattle" and remarks in the following paragraph: "How little better is either the civil or religious state of the poor American Indians! That is, the miserable remains of them; for in some provinces not one of them is left to breathe."[3]

If we hope to understand the relation of Methodism and liberation movements in Latin America, we must focus on the two most important events in Latin America in the first half of the nineteenth century. The balance of power in Europe had changed; Spain and Portugal had lost their leadership, which moved to the North—Great Britain and, at a lower level, the Netherlands and France. The United States was emerging as a significant power and the landlords and merchants in Latin America needed to jump over the walls of Spain and Portugal and negotiate directly with the new powers. They were supported by a new intellectual elite that had drunk the inebriating wines of modernity. The common people—indigenous, "criollos," or "mestizos"—could easily be drafted for a war of independence. So, by the end of the 1840s, practically all Latin American countries were free nations. A new relation with European (mostly Protestant) countries was established and, though the Roman Catholic Church continued to be the only authorized church, Protestant business agents were given a certain controlled and circumscribed freedom to practice their faith. The first "liberation movement" had been successful. But soon a second one was afoot: the younger intelligentsia wanted to push liberation to embrace values of the French Revolution and the United States War for Independence: democracy, freedom of thought, industrial growth—in fact, modernity. Liberal governments began to take control of the new countries and to seek a new emancipation from traditional semi-feudal monopoly, cultural

---

3. "In Hispaniola," he continues, "when the Christians came thither first, there were three millions of inhabitants. Scarce twelve thousands of them now survive." Sermon 69, "The Imperfection of Human Knowledge," §II.6, *Works* 2:580. Wesley's understanding of the indigenous people oscillates, sometimes extolling their virtues, honesty, and nobility, in an almost Rousseaunian vein, and other times horrified by their brutality. He became very interested in the indigenous people in the south of North America, whom he had expected to evangelize, but did not seem to have known about the indigenous cultures and empires in and south of what is now Mexico.

and religious domination, and a premodern economy. The 1850s and 1860s saw the triumph of the liberal elite. With them came religious tolerance and eventually religious freedom. The first Protestants to enter under these conditions were "immigrants" at different levels—workers, farmers, administrators of foreign companies, technicians, and others—who in most cases transplanted their religious affiliation, and their missionary churches, mostly from the U.S. and Great Britain, which came to evangelize the native population. Of the latter, the Methodists were among the first.

When Wesley Arrived in Latin America

Wesley came to Latin America in many different garbs, which can be helpfully gathered into three distinct waves of migration:[4] (1) After the 1820s the U.S. Methodist churches began to send missionaries to Haiti (1823), the Dominican Republic (1834), Uruguay and Argentina (1835), Brazil (1836), Mexico (1844–45), Cuba (1873), Paraguay and Peru (1886), Bolivia and Venezuela (1890), and Puerto Rico and Costa Rica (1900). By the end of the century, The Methodist Episcopal Church, North or South, was present in practically all of Latin America. (2) This "classical" Wesleyanism would represent less than a third of the total Wesleyan family today. The second wave involved the churches born from the Holiness movements in the U.S. in the period between 1870 and 1910: the Church of God (Anderson, Indiana), the Salvation Army, the Church of the Nazarene, the Pilgrim Holiness Church, the Christian and Missionary Alliance, and several small churches organized in the U.S. or Great Britain. By 1914 all of these churches were present in Latin America. Their evangelistic commitment made them a significant presence, and their theological influence permeated to some extent all evangelical Christianity in Latin America. (3) The third wave appeared in 1909 in the Methodist church of the port city of Valparaiso (Chile) when a Methodist missionary—Willis Hoover—who had an expectation of a new Pentecost, came in contact with

---

4. This brief description is a summary of a paper prepared for the Rio de Janeiro Assembly of the World Methodist Council in 1997. I have tried to offer an account and interpretation of the Protestant presence in Latin America in *Faces of Latin American Protestantism* (Grand Rapids: Wm. B. Eerdman, 1997).

the recent Pentecostal events at the Azusa Street church (California, U.S.) and fueled and gave shape to the charismatic movement in his and other Methodist parishes. As they were expelled from Methodism they initiated the Methodist Pentecostal Church and the Evangelical Pentecostal Church, which today make up 75 percent of the total evangelical population of Chile. Under different names, Pentecostalism today represents the majority of Latin American Protestantism, and other churches in the Wesleyan tradition represent probably 10 percent to 15 percent of the total Protestant population of the continent.

What has been the impact of these Wesleyan churches in Latin America? There are at least three areas in which Methodism has had a limited but significant presence in the religious, social, and cultural life of the continent: (1) Methodism—particularly the "classical" Methodist churches—had a great concern for the educational and cultural contribution that they could make in these countries, which they saw as victims of backward political, social, and religious influences. Education would be the answer, so they created a number of "model" educational institutions at the secondary and university levels in the hope that a modern, progressive, and at the same time ethically and evangelically inspired education could give the new elite the kind of formation that would produce a modern, democratic, and ethically healthy leading class. (2) However, in both the classical churches and the later holiness and Pentecostal churches, Methodists' dominant concern was evangelization. For many Methodist leaders this was closely related to the educational dimension because conversion to the gospel would free people from a passive, almost superstitious religion and create "new human beings," transformed, morally healthy, responsible, and socially active citizens. (3) This task was successful more in the lower and low middle-class sectors, in popular workers' neighborhoods, among recently arrived worker immigrants, or among people who had moved from the countryside to peripheral city quarters. Besides focusing on the evangelistic task, Methodists also created elementary schools, medical services, and other expressions of social concern.

How *Wesleyan* were Wesleyan churches in Latin America? This question is not merely rhetorical; it has to do with the nature of evangelization and the social and ethical understanding of the faith. Several points need to be considered in answering the question. (1) Latin America received a *mediated* Wesley. It inherited much of the early Methodist evangelistic zeal, it reproduced some of its organizational features—certainly a very positive stabilizing factor—and it showed an active social and educational concern. But all of this was filtered by the "American experience," and more precisely by the Wesleyanism of the second American revival and the Holiness movement. A look at the hymnody, in which the contributions of Charles, John, and Samuel Wesley are reduced to a minimum, offers a good indicator of the kind of evangelical theology that fed the Methodist faith in Latin America. (2) This influence of Anglo-Saxon late evangelicalism has continued to shape much of the theology of the people, even in Methodist churches that officially adhere to the classical articles and confessional documents of Wesleyan origins. The polemical conditions in which these churches grew—struggling for their right to exist and to evangelize—strengthened the anti-sacramental and anti-liturgical tendencies already present in that late evangelicalism. Likewise, the opposition which U.S. evangelicalism developed against social concerns in the early decades of the twentieth century (what Moberg has called "the Great Reversal")[5] and their reaction to "the social gospel" had a strong influence in the self-understanding of Wesleyan evangelical churches in Latin America (perhaps with the partial exception of those churches which were related to The Methodist Episcopal Church). To be sure, many local churches helped the poor at local level—many of them were themselves poor—and supported schools and orphanages. But this service was considered "accidental and subordinate" and not integrated into their evangelistic and theological self-understanding. (3) Wesley himself—his story, writings, theology—has been largely absent from Latin American Wesleyanism. Only the *Standard Sermons* and a few scattered writings were translated and, until recently, biographic or theological books about him could be counted on the fingers of one hand. In fact, one could say that Wesley had been (probably unconsciously) sequestered. In some recent workshops with ministers of churches of Wesleyan origin, frequently from rural, small villages, or poor areas in Peru, Bolivia, and Chile, the

---

5. See David O. Moberg, *The Great Reversal: Evangelism versus Social Concern* (Philadelphia: J. B. Lippincott, 1972).

reading of varied Wesley writings—hymns, appeals, thoughts, even sections of the *Journals*—found a spontaneous response which does not come so much from their previous theological education—which rather moved in an opposite direction—but from the natural relation which they find with their everyday pastoral experiences. (4) Although these comments are to some extent generalizations, on the whole evangelical—including Wesleyan—theology as it came to, and developed in, Latin America has suffered from a typical late evangelical reductionism. What is sometimes praised as a christological concentration becomes a one-sided, subjectivistic piety restricted to an experience of conversion and an individualistic (and frequently moralistic) sanctification. To be sure, the life of evangelical Christians and churches is much richer than this picture—their lives, service, evangelistic passion, and compassion far exceed the limitations of their theology. But precisely this introduces the ambiguities, limitations, and contradictions that are clearly visible and seriously impair their mission and testimony.

Wesleyanism at the Opening of the Twenty-first Century

Can we speak of Latin American Wesleyanism as a "liberation movement" as we look at what it has been and done along this brief trip through the nineteenth and twentieth centuries? This question became an existential dilemma for many Methodists in "mainline" Latin American Methodism (basically, those in the Methodist Episcopal Church). The liberal modernizing project to which they had contributed included a social dimension that these Methodists, in different degrees and ways, had made their own, in many cases in the direction of "the Social Gospel." But the project, which after World War II, and with the support and participation of the U.S.—Good Neighbor Policy, Alliance for Progress—rested on the "development" programs was, from the beginning of the 1960s, clearly floundering. North African and Latin American sociologists and economists denounced "dependence" as the basic reason for this failure and the "Third World" movements demanded a new kind of relation between "developed" and so called "developing" (in fact, "under-developing") countries. Adding to their disease, these Methodist churches had joined the ecumenical movement (the World Council of Churches) in which the social question, the idea of "nation building," and the struggles for liberation in Asia and Africa had become burning issues.

How could younger Methodist men and women interpret the role of their churches' alliance with the modernizing model? Was it not precisely this project that had placed the Latin American countries on the periphery of the new configuration of economic power and in the orbit of the political power of the North Atlantic world in its capitalist expansion? In other words, we began to feel that our Methodism (in fact, Protestantism) had been, not necessarily in a simplistic or Machiavellian sense, but as a religious dimension, a partner in a global project, what we usually call "the "colonial pact." This precipitated a crisis of identity in the Protestant sectors that became conscious of the situation. It is quite understandable that this produced in many young Protestants a movement of rejection of this past, even more when they saw their churches and leaders not infrequently allying themselves with reactionary oligarchies or with the small urban instrumental middle class, or becoming ghettos alienated from the concerns of the society where they themselves live. Many of us, however, while we shared the concern, would see this history in a more dialectical way, in which the "modernizing" project has to be understood as a negation of a feudalistic colonial society, a reactionary ideology, and a backward looking religion. In other terms, Protestantism was a *subversive* element in terms of the traditional Latin American society. Its values, goals, and attitudes belonged to a different order. Even in their simplicity, for these "converts," the gospel meant freedom.

If this is so, our rejection of the present order is not merely a negation of the existing conditions, it is a movement toward a new project of freedom. Latin America has to move beyond its "liberal" history in the double Hegelian sense of "assuming" and "negating." This is not easy because Latin America has not lived this stage as a self-generated project in which we have been a fully active subject but as a project induced from outside, in the framework of neocolonial relations of dependence. It is, however, a transition without return, which has to be evaluated as a necessary moment of our historical process. The hypothetical alternative of "returning" to another imaginary past history is a kind of idealism that has no use at all. The blind refusal of that time in our continent, as if we could erase it and return to an idyllic past that in fact has never existed (the colonial society? the pre-Colombian world?), is a dangerous romanticism. The only possible route is to move forward, through this crisis, to a new moment in history.

Before turning to a discussion of what this means today, in concrete terms, for the Wesleyan people and churches, we need to take a moment to consider the present Latin American situation as we enter the twenty-first century. The crisis of the 1960s, which we discussed earlier, was followed by three very important "moments" which are essential for discerning the tasks for the future.

(1) The crisis of the development project and the conviction that the future of Latin American nations—and particularly of the poor, the "nonperson," the "crucified people"—demanded a radical transformation of society at the economic, political, cultural,. and religious levels—a revolutionary change, in the sense of not merely partial changes but a breaking away from the present organization of society, are the factors that precipitated revolutionary movements of different types during the late 1960s and the early 1970s. At the theological level, this meant a rereading and reinterpretation of the biblical and theological tradition which is usually called "liberation theology," in which, to be sure with certain differences, many Methodist young people and theologians were active participants.[6] At the pastoral level, however, this theology was not simply a theological exercise but a new way of "doing theology," born or nourished from a religious awakening in which many "Base Ecclesial Communities" emerged among poor people, mainly in the Roman Catholic Church but, in some cases, in cooperation with Protestant (in many cases Methodist) communities.

(2) Parallel to these movements, the dominant economic interests in Latin America—allied to the Latin American military and trained, organized continentally and supported politically and economically by the U.S. ideology and policy of National Security—

---

6. Among many expressions of this concern in Methodism we find a number of publications such as Theo Tschuy, ed., *Explosives Lateinamerika: Der Protestantsmos inmitten der sozialen Revolution* (Berlin: Lettner-Verlag, 1969); José Duque, ed., *La tradición protestante en la teología latinoamericana: Primer intento—lectura de la tradición metodista* (San José, Costa Rica: 1983); José Míguez Bonino, Carmerlo Alvarez, et al., *Protestantismo y liberalismo en América Latina* (San José, Costa Rica: DEI, 1983); and Theodore Runyon, et al., *Theology, Politics and Peace* (Maryknoll, N.Y.: Orbis Books, 1989).

launched a war of annihilation, not only of armed revolutionary movements but of all ideological, political, intellectual, or religious expressions of protest or demands of change. Country after country in Latin America was taken over in the late 1960s and the 1970s by military governments that launched the systematic destruction of all opposition. A number of Protestant churches, most of them related to the Ecumenical Movement—among them a significant Methodist presence, together with Roman Catholics in some of the countries—were at the head of "Human Rights" movements and not a few paid with their lives for their participation in this struggle for peace. Liberation struggle meant in these years simply "the defense of human life."

(3) By the end of the 1980s the economic and political control of the Latin American countries was totally in the hands of the international economic powers and their political instruments of domination—specifically conservative forces in the U.S. (which, in terms of economic policies and international relations with Latin America, did not change significantly during the Clinton Administration). The results for the conditions of the people were similar in all of Latin America: pauperization, exclusion, high and rising cost of living, growing illiteracy and infant mortality, rising unemployment indexes. These conditions existed even in countries like Argentina and Uruguay, which had been known for their relatively high standards of living. As the situation becomes more and more critical, large sectors of the lower middle classes, both specialized workers and white-collar employees and professionals, fall into structural poverty. The well-known recent popular unrest in Argentina, whether it takes the form of poor people's plundering of supermarkets and stores, of workers blocking streets and roads, or of the middle class protesting in the streets (what is called the "*cacerolazos*": banging pots and saucepans in the streets) have already forced four presidents to resign in two months. Every new program that has been tried sinks under the weight of the demands of the International Monetary Fund, the U.S. government's conditions, the pressure of international banking and transnational corporations, and—why should we deny it—also the corruption and ineffectiveness of our political parties and politicians.

What Can "Radical Methodism" Mean in That Situation?

This is the challenge. For Latin American Wesleyanism, movement forward through this crisis (Brazilians would call it *caminhada*—choosing a path to follow, a walk toward a goal) necessarily involves several things: (1) rereading the Wesleyan tradition, both in the sense of recovering the values that had been ignored or distorted in the type of Wesleyanism that we have received, and reinterpreting them in the context of our present situation; (2) doing this task within the framework of Latin American Protestantism and the Latin American religious history as a whole—to try to define a self-sufficient and independent "Wesleyan project" for Latin America is dangerous nonsense; and (3) relating our theological, pastoral, and social task to the conditions, the struggles, the basic needs, and the projects of the Latin American people, particularly those who are suffering most from the present conditions.

There can be no movement forward if the issues involved are addressed simply as theoretical or intellectual problems. They must be addressed by a "trial and error" praxis. And this praxis cannot consist of haphazard and arbitrary actions but has to be accompanied and supported by reflection, analysis, consultation, and dialogue, as well as by love, solidarity, and prayer. I will close this somewhat unorganized essay by mentioning some of the signs that can give us, in all their precariousness, lines of thought and action that may help Wesleyanism to be of service to our peoples.

1. What is our strength and where are our weaknesses? Jesus reminds us that a king must "count his troops" before launching a war (Luke 14:31), and Paul prays for Christians to have a "love" that is informed by "knowledge" (Phil. 1:9). The classical Methodist churches have gained in Latin America a certain recognition through the work and service of many of their leaders at critical moments. But the more charismatic expressions of Wesleyanism—particularly, but not exclusively, in Wesleyan Pentecostalism—have been closer to the poor because most of them belong to these sectors of society and have shared in their need and suffering. Can we amalgamate these two dimensions of the Wesleyan tradition and share this gift of God with similar and diverse gifts of other Protestant and evangelical sisters and brothers? There are already, in different places of our countries, good

examples of this kind of service. We need to find ways of sharing these experiences and strengthening each other.

2. Methodists and other evangelicals—and certainly also other Christians—have been and are active in social, cultural, and political activity, participating in popular movements for change. A love that does not find ways of serving can hardly be recognized as Christian. This has been a fundamental conviction in the Wesleyan tradition. But Wesley would at the same time remind us that the richest and most important gift that we can share is our faith, our hope in Christ. Our presence in Latin American life is a witness of faith in the gospel. The thirst for the presence of the Spirit is as deep and strong in our people—and very particularly in those whom our present society marginalizes and negates—as is the hunger for food and shelter. In order to be able to stand and fight for the social, economical, and political changes that are needed, the poor need the strength that comes from the assurance that they receive and share the power, the certainty, the purpose of a God who is above them, with them, and in them. Our "works" as Christians, like Jesus' miracles, are not the magic that we simply receive and enjoy, but the "sign" that intends to strengthen and move us to action. The religious dimension—if we can use this rather abstract expression—is at the heart of our partici-pation in a "liberation movement." In this sense, our churches have to develop a "pastoral service" in the sense of offering support, com-fort, courage, and hope to the abandoned, excluded, bewildered, and hopeless multitudes of people who—as in the time of Jesus—are "harassed and helpless, like sheep without a shepherd" (Matt. 9:37).

3. During the period of military governments and in the crises of the present, many Methodist leaders have played, within an ecu-menical context, an important prophetic role. More recently, in some of our countries—Chile, Argentina, and Ecuador, for exam-ple—such witness has not been limited to an elite but has been generated from the membership of churches and congregations which themselves belong to "the margin." And, in some cases, this has happened in the context of, and as participation in, larger expressions of the people's need and protest. Recent evangelical public demonstrations, gathering in some cases hundreds of thou-sands, have expressed, as an act of prophetic faith, the concerns, the needs, and the demands of the poor. Moreover, the thousands of local initiatives to generate from the bottom of society local

organizations to offer "alternatives" to the economic domination from the top frequently include the active presence of evangelicals. In such movements there is a promising encounter of marginals, workers, and middle-class people who demand and try to anticipate a radical transformation of the social, political, and economic structures of our present societies. There is much in the early Wesleyan tradition, and in the social movements which sometimes emerged from it, that can help such movements.

4. The unbearable and increasing pressure from the transnational economic forces, sustained and abetted by the most powerful nations—particularly the U.S.—and their allies in the poor nations—banks, local representatives of transnational interests, and corrupt politicians—is driving the people to the verge of destruction. There are signs that movements and efforts of resistance to this "genocide" are likely to be met by brutal repression from inside and outside the countries. We may be moving to the critical point in which the Christian churches—if they want to be even minimally worthy of their name—will have to declare a *status confessionis* or denounce a "heresy," in which not only the ethical responsibility but faith itself is at stake. For Wesleyans, this is the position that Wesley took with relation to slavery and slave trading, basing opposition not only on acts of mercy, not even only as a question of human justice, but as a crime against God—a mortal sin—in the person of God's human creation, the free and responsible human being.

5. Finally, we must recognize that our inability in the past to offer our people an adequate understanding of "liberation" is also due to a partialized and therefore distorted theology. Fundamental theological concepts like the trinitarian nature of God, redemption, and the work of the Holy Spirit, which are so central in Wesley's theology, have been boxed into individualistic, otherworldly dimensions which make Christians and churches unable to see their relation to social, economic, political life.[7] For all the limitations of Wesley's conservative tradition, he was always trying to understand and include these social, economic, and political dimensions in the responsibilities of Christian life. This is a part of our heritage well worth recovering.

---

7. Fortunately we can refer now to an increasing number of theological publications that try to recover this tradition. Among others, articles in M. Douglas Meeks, ed., *Trinity, Community, and Power* (Nashville: Kingswood Books, 2000); Richard P. Heitzenrater, ed., *The Poor and the People Called Methodists* (Nashville: Kingswood Books, 2002); as well as other articles in the present publication.

CONCLUSION
JOERG RIEGER
JOHN VINCENT

We hope that we have shown that you can be both radical and Methodist—or Methodist and radical. But what are the hopes for rejuvenating the tradition? Will Methodists bite? Will Radicals believe? And what about God?

Will Methodists bite? Perhaps they would if they knew the option. The prospect of a radical, nonestablishment, discipleship-based critical engagement at the creative, neglected edges of our contemporary world is, we believe, just what is needed by the world today—a world too often wedded to narrow self-interest, the hegemony of the rich, and world dictatorship by a threatening, unacceptable so-called "Christian" West. The followers of the social entrepreneur, John Wesley, with his army of homemade saints and communitarians, singing their songs of Zion on earth, must be the counterhegemonic vanguards of new futures, based on heroic contrariness in the midst of all times, and especially now.

Will radicals believe? Yes, provided we keep that old, contrary nickname of Methodist, and provided we now look for allies, not in the conformist, hegemonic major denominations, hurtling into united oblivion, but in the outsiders, the alternative communities, the social experimenters, and the world of the common people. The world of the small, the alternative, the heroic, the significant, is still there, waiting for its constant resurrection and reincarnation among the "not many wise, not many powerful, not many top people" (1 Cor. 1:26, author's paraphrase), of which we can number the radical Methodists, in Wesley's day and often since, and, we trust, around the corner in your communities and ours, now.

And what about God? None of this will mean anything unless God in Christ through the Holy Spirit is the first radical. This volume is ultimately about God. It is about the One for whom "the last shall be the first and the first shall be the last" (Matt. 20:16, Rieger), about the One to whom we owe our radical commitment and discipleship (Vincent), about the One who "has broken down the dividing wall" and "the hostility between us" (Eph. 2:14, Jennings), about the One whose radical love defies slavery, racism, and exclusion (Young), about the One who is the God of life who resists death and suffering (Recinos), about the One who promotes justice and healing (Andrew Sung Park), about the One who opens our ears and makes us receptive (Chopp), about the One whose concerns are wider than those of the established church (Hatcher), about the One who radically transforms both the church and the world and continues to be at work there (Mayson), about the One whose love for the world inspires our love and leads us to mutuality (Oduyoye), about the One whose presence within us makes all the difference (J. C. Park), about the One who makes us read differently (Havea), and about the One who brings about true liberation that can no longer be boxed in (Míguez Bonino).

It all hangs together. All that we do is related to our images and visions of God. Where do such images and visions come from? Like in Wesley's days, we will only come to know who God is by joining in God's work in community with others, particularly with those on the margins whom we often overlook. As we enter into relationships of solidarity, listening, and respect with other people, both at home and halfway around the globe, new relationships of solidarity, listening, and respect with the divine Other become available that continue to surprise us. It is then that lives change, that those in positions of power and control can learn to let go, and that those in positions without power gather strength. May God keep us on the move.

CONTRIBUTORS

Rebecca S. Chopp is an ordained elder and member of the Kansas East Conference of The United Methodist Church. Recently named President of Colgate University in Hamilton, New York, she has also taught at Candler School of Theology, Emory University, has served as provost of Emory University, and was dean and professor of theology at Yale Divinity School. Her publications include *Saving Work: Feminist Practices of Theological Education* (1995), *The Power to Speak: Feminism, Language, God* (1989), and *The Praxis of Suffering: An Interpretation of Liberation and Political Theologies* (1986). She was coeditor of *Differing Horizons: Feminist Theory and Theology* (1997), and *Reconstructing Christian Theology* (1999). She has also served as President of the American Academy of Religion.

Stephen G. Hatcher is an ordained minister in the British Methodist Conference and Director of The Englesea Brook Chapel and Museum, Englesea Brook, Crewe, Cheshire, Great Britain. His Ph.D. was on *The Origins and Rise of Primitive Methodism (1990)*. He is a frequent lecturer and resource on working-class Methodism, past and present.

Jione Havea was ordained by The Methodist Church in Tonga and is now Lecturer of Biblical Studies at United Theological College and Charles Sturt University in Australia. His articles that offer approaches/readings similar to his chapter in this volume are "Shifting the Boundaries: house of God and the politics of reading," *The Pacific Journal of Theology* 2.16 (1996): 55-71, and *"Tau Lave!* (Let's talk)," *The Pacific Journal of Theology* 2.20 (1998): 63-73.

Theodore W. (Ted) Jennings Jr., ordained elder and member of the Florida Annual Conference of The United Methodist Church, is Professor of Biblical and Constructive Theology at the Chicago Theological Seminary. He has also taught at Candler School of Theology and at the Seminario Metodista de Mexico in Mexico City. In addition to numerous articles in scholarly and ecclesiastical journals, he has written nine books including: *Beyond Theism* (1985), *Life as Worship* (1982), *Good News to the Poor: John Wesley's Evangelical Economics* (1990), and *Loyalty to God* (1992). Ted has also lectured widely in the U.S., Europe, Latin America, and Asia. He initiated the Chicago Theological Seminary's Gay and Lesbian Studies program in 1991 and has served as consultant to the Task Force of the United Methodist Council of Bishops Initiative on Children and Poverty since 1996.

Cedric Mayson is a supernumerary (retired) minister of The Methodist Church of South Africa (ordained in 1958), and works full time at the Religious Desk in the Johannesburg Headquarters of the African National Congress (ANC), the governing political party in South Africa. Recently he has worked to initiate a national Moral Regeneration Movement, incorporating government, all political parties and religions, and all sectors of civil society. His chapter "Faith in the Context of God-less-ness" is included in *Towards an Agenda for Contextual Theology* (2001).

José Míguez Bonino is an ordained presbyter of the Iglesia Evangélica Metodista Argentina, and Emeritus Professor of Systematic Theology and Ethics of ISEDET (Protestant School of Theology in Buenos Aires, Argentina). He has taught in many countries. Most recently, in 2001, he served as Monrad Visiting Professor of World Christianity at Harvard Divinity School. He is copresident of the Permanent Assembly for Human Rights in Argentina, and an elected member of the National Constitutional Assembly. He has authored several books, including *Toward a Christian Political Ethics* (1982), *Faces of Jesus: Latin American Christologies* (1984), and *Faces of Latin American Protestantism* (1997).

Mercy Amba Oduyoye is a Methodist lay preacher and a theologian from Ghana. Former Deputy General Secretary of the World

Council of Churches, she is now Director of the Institute of African Women in Religion and Culture, Trinity Theological Seminary, Legon, Ghana. Her recent publications include *Hearing and Knowing: Theological Reflections on Christianity in Africa* (1986), *Daughters of Anowa: African Women and Patriarchy* (1995), and *Introducing African Women's Theology* (2001).

Andrew Sung Park, ordained elder and member of the California-Nevada Annual Conference of The United Methodist Church, is Professor of Theology at United Theological Seminary, Dayton, Ohio, and has taught at Claremont School of Theology, California. His publications include *The Wounded Heart of God: the Asian Concept of Han and the Christian Concept of Sin* (1993), *Racial Conflict and Healing* (1996), and *The Other Side of Sin* (coeditor with Susan Nelson, 2001).

Jong Chun Park is an ordained minister of the Korean Methodist Church and Professor of Systematic Theology at the Methodist Theological Seminary in Seoul, Korea. He has taught Asian Theology as Visiting Professor at Iliff School of Theology and at Candler School of Theology. In addition to three books and many articles in Korean, he has published *Crawl with God and Dance in the Spirit! A Creative Formation of the Korean Theology of the Spirit* (1998). He is a member of the executive committee of the Oxford Institute of Methodist Theological Studies, and a member of the executive committee of the World Methodist Council.

Harold J. Recinos, an ordained elder and member of the Baltimore-Washington Annual Conference of The United Methodist Church, is Professor of Church and Society at Perkins School of Theology, Southern Methodist University. He has also taught on the faculty of Wesley Seminary in Washington, D.C. His writing includes *Hear the Cry! A Latino Pastor Challenges the Church* (1989), *Jesus Weeps: Global Encounters on our Doorstep* (1992), and *Who Comes in the Name of the Lord? Jesus at the Margins* (1997).

Joerg Rieger, an ordained elder, raised in the German United Methodist Church and now member of the North Texas Annual Conference of The United Methodist Church, is Associate Professor of Systematic Theology at Perkins School of Theology, Southern Methodist University. He is author of articles in English and German and of *Remember the Poor: The Challenge to Theology in the Twenty-first Century* (1998), and *God and the Excluded: Visions and Blindspots in Contemporary Theology* (2001). He is editor of *Liberating the Future: God, Mammon, and Theology* (1998), *Theology from the Belly of the Whale: A Frederick Herzog Reader* (1999), and *Opting for the Margins: Postmodernity and Liberation in Christian Theology* (2003).

John Vincent is an ordained minister in the British Methodist Conference. He is Founder and Director Emeritus, Urban Theology Unit, and Honorary Lecturer at Sheffield University. He was president of the British Methodist Conference from 1989 to1990. He writes on Methodism in *Christ and Methodism: Towards a New Christianity for a New Age* (1965) and *OK, Let's Be Methodists* (1983), on discovering a contemporary Jesus in *Secular Christ* (1968), *Radical Jesus* (1986), and *Journey: Explorations in Discipleship* (2001), and on urban ministry in *Into the City* (1982), and *Hope from the City* (2000). With Chris Rowland, he edits the biannual "British Liberation Theology" series, and continues to pioneer inner-city projects and houses through the Ashram Community.

Josiah U. Young III, ordained elder in the New York Conference of The United Methodist Church, is Professor of Systematic Theology at Wesley Theological Seminary in Washington, D.C. He is the author of many articles and books, including *A Pan-African Theology: Providence and the Legacies of the Ancestors* (1992), and *No Difference in the Fare: Dietrich Bonhoeffer and the Problem of Racism* (1998). Professor Young is interested in the problem of theodicy, the praxis of social and economic justice, and Africana spirituality, as is borne out by his forthcoming book, *Dogged Strength Within the Veil: Africana Spirituality and the Mysterious Love of God.*

Index

Printed in the United States
15898LVS00004B/202-255